QUEERFULLY
AND
WONDERFULLY
MADE

A Guide for LGBTQ+ Christian Teens

Published in 2020 by Beaming Books, an imprint of
1517 Media. All rights reserved. No part of this book may be
reproduced without the written permission of the publisher. Email
copyright@1517.media. Printed in the USA.

26 25 24 23 22 21 20   1 2 3 4 5 6 7 8

Paperback ISBN: 978-1-5064-6524-1
Ebook ISBN: 978-1-5064-6668-2

Cover and interior design by Emily Harris
Illustrations by Shelby Pearson
Page layout by Kristin Miller
Editorial support: Lauren Welch, Erik Ullestad

Library of Congress Cataloging-in-Publication Data
A CIP record is on file with the Library of Congress.
VN0004589; 9781506465241; JUL2020

Beaming Books
510 Marquette Avenue
Minneapolis, MN 55402
Beamingbooks.com

QUEERFULLY
AND
WONDERFULLY
MADE

A Guide for LGBTQ+ Christian Teens

Edited by **Leigh Finke**
with an introduction by
Jennifer Knapp

beaming
books
MINNEAPOLIS

CONTRIBUTORS

ISAAC ARCHULETA has a Master of Arts in Clinical Mental Health Counseling, and established a nationally recognized counseling practice devoted to helping the LGBTQ+ community thrive.

CARLA BARNHILL brings to this project more than three decades of working with teenagers. They are among her favorite people. Carla edits and writes and tries to make the world a little better from her home in Minneapolis.

REV. ASHLEY DETAR BIRT is the Pastoral Fellow for Youth and Families at Rutgers Presbyterian Church in New York City. She also serves on the board of More Light Presbyterians, an LGBTQ+ organization within the PC(USA). Her ministry focuses on children, families, and racial and social justice.

K. AMANDA MEISENHEIMER is a minister and former public-school teacher. She specializes in communication and advocacy for children. She and her two children make their home in Manhattan.

ROSS MURRAY is the founding director of The Naming Project, a Christian ministry for LGBTQ+ youth, as well as the senior director of the GLAAD Media Institute. He is a deacon in the Evangelical Lutheran Church in America, with a calling to LGBTQ+ advocacy and ministry between the LGBTQ+ and faith communities.

SHELBY PEARSON is an artist based in Minneapolis. Whether through illustration or animation, she thrives on bringing joy to others through visual storytelling.

GERMONO TOUSSAINT is a multi–award-winning playwright, composer, and producer, and an African American, same-gender-loving, ordained minister. He is the founding artistic director of A Mile In My Shoes Inc. and one of the founding playwrights of the Obie Award–winning The Fire This Time Festival. Due to his upbringing in the often-contradictory world of basement parties and the black church, his work focuses on how people navigate the sacred and the profane, the flesh and the spirit, or the natural and the supernatural.

CONTENTS

FOREWORD

by Jennifer Knapp

Let's face it: we live in a world full of people who assume you are straight.

Unless you tell them otherwise, anyway. And they'll assume that each person's gender identity is easily judged at first (anatomical) sight. You may have even made these assumptions about yourself, going with the flow, until you began to realize that you aren't exactly in the center of this otherwise straight, cisgender narrative.

This is because heteronormativity—the belief that cisgender, heterosexual people are "normal" and anyone else is not—often actively seeks to exclude the LGBTQ+ experience. Coming out as queer says, "Hold on a minute. That's not exactly how we all work. That's not how I work!"

It is only when we begin to openly talk about the many different ways in which we experience our gender identity and our expressions of sexuality that we begin to see the fact that we are all queerfully and wonderfully made.

In order to be authentic in the world, we find there are times where it is important to be vocal about the facts about who we are. Rather than relying on other people to figure it out, or to assume, instead we have to do a little work in communicating who it is that we are, what we need, and share something of ourselves

And when enough people disrupt the norms, a time comes when these assumptions need to be addressed.

But coming out is more than just sharing the facts of our sexual orientation and gender identity. I believe that coming out is rooted in our need to be connected. Every human being wants to be appreciated and recognized for who they are, inside and out. Every new relationship starts with sharing information about our person in ways that draw us toward one another. We form bonds and determine our levels of intimacy and reliability with one another. We reach out in order to know others and to be known by others. Because of this, disclosing one's gender identity and/or sexual orientation becomes profoundly important. Coming out not only breaks the cycle of heteronormative assumption, it also lets us experience integrity and dignity because we have welcomed something deeply true and personal about ourselves.

It takes courage to set the record straight to those around us who assume we are not who we are.

I was in my late twenties before I began to pay attention to my sexual orientation, and it wasn't until I was in my thirties that I felt comfortable enough to share it with (literally) the world. In a lot of ways, I'm envious that this book wasn't around when I was growing up.

I often felt alone. I felt like I was on a road I knew led to somewhere, but the road was so overgrown with misinformation and lies that it seemed I would never find safe passage. Finding safe passage took coming out. It took admitting that I had to learn about sex when I thought I knew all there was to know. It took giving myself grace and permission to take a path that differed from the heterosexual path I had always known.

I couldn't do this in isolation. I needed help along the way. Help that you can find in this book.

As you begin reading *Queerfully and Wonderfully Made*, take a moment to recognize the effort it's taken you to get to here. Our social and religious communities can take for granted how easy it is to find information and examples of what it's like to be straight or cisgender. Tragically, the history of imposed silence and invisibility experienced by LGBTQ+ people has made it very difficult to do the same.

Finding queer connections, role models, and resources that center our particularities has never been easy, especially for those in a Christian environment that might withhold the love and support you need. It's not uncommon for faith communities to name our differences and set us apart as peculiar people. The premise of this book is that LGBTQ+ people are not peculiar at all, but rather, that our needs are particular. Particular because what counts as good guidance for a straight person doesn't always work for a queer person. Such a claim is not controversial, but simply a recognition of the reality of an LGBTQ+ person at the start of their journey.

You may have already discovered that there's a whole new language to learn. There's LGBTQ+…Plus what, exactly? Words like *heteronormativity, cisgender, pansexual,* or *nonbinary* take some getting used to if you haven't heard or used them before. But this shared language is part of our community's connective tissue. Getting on the same page with our language and definitions can serve as a starting point for feeling less alone.

Maybe "gay" doesn't fit you any more than "straight" does? Perhaps coming out is too much of a leap for you right now and you simply can't imagine how to begin this conversation. Maybe you've already come out, to a friend or a parent, and now you're looking for reliable resources to help you process the wide range of questions running through your mind? Speaking up and reaching for what you need isn't always easy, but it is why we are gathering in this place! Drawing from the wisdom and experience of LGBTQ+ Christians who have come before you, *Queerfully and Wonderfully Made* will help guide you on a journey of self-discovery as you seek to gain confidence in faithfully understanding your sexuality and gender. Additionally, it may prove useful to share this book with your loved ones, who may be on their own journey toward acceptance and affirmation.

Remember that life (and faith) is a journey and that coming out is a *process*. A process that allows us to be honest and responsible for our desires, our sense of self, our relationships with others, and our actions. In this sense, coming out is an act of a mature faith that is always learning.

This is all serious work, to be sure, but don't forget to have a little fun too. It's a wonderful thing to be curious and queer. Find joy in talking about sexuality and gender. *Blushing is beautiful!* From the questions that make you nervously giggle, but you still want to ask, to the questions about how to deal with churches that make you second-guess your own self-worth. Have fun, learn, and know: You *are* worthy, holy, and free, our LGBTQ+ beloved!

Faithfully yours,
Jennifer Knapp

A NOTE ON LANGUAGE

This is a book for queer Christians. If you're reading it, you probably identify in some way with one or both of those words: *queer* and *Christian*. And those words are whoppers. So before we start, let's break them down a bit to make sure you know exactly what we're talking about.

QUEER

We are using the term *queer* in this book as shorthand for the entire spectrum of LGBTQ+ identities: gay, lesbian, bi, pan, ace, aro. Trans, genderfluid, genderqueer. Two-spirit, questioning, nonbinary. All of us. We're here. We're queer.

The word *queer* covers a lot of people. And not all folks are queer in the same way (what fun would that be?). One big distinction in queer identities that you'll find in this book is between sexual orientation (who you are attracted to) and gender identity (who you are). We'll try our best to be specific about our language when we're talking explicitly about gender or sexuality. But we are using *queer*, generally, as shorthand for all of us.

CHRISTIAN

One thing the words *queer* and *Christian* have in common: there are seemingly countless ways to identify with them. So, whether you call yourself Christian, Lutheran, nondenominational, Baptist, Catholic, Evangelical, a Christ-follower, a disciple, a believer, or just a person with a fondness for Jesus, we're talking about you. Or maybe you're questioning whether you're even Christian at all. That's okay, too.

But we have to use words or we can't get anywhere. So for the purpose of this book, when we say *Christian*, we're talking about the whole culture of Christianity. There's so much diversity represented in that word that we'd need twenty volumes of this book to get into the nitty-gritty of different versions of the faith. Not to mention the fact that churches are changing their approach to queerness all the time. Your religious context might teach that being queer is fabulous and part of God's plan, or it might teach that being queer—or even thinking queer thoughts—is a sin. Most likely your religious context is somewhere in between. Whatever your relationship is to Christianity right now, whatever faith community you belong to, we've made this book for you.

So. Queer + Christian = you. Got it? Okay. Let's get to your questions.

HOW DO I EVEN KNOW WHO I AM?

If you're reading this book, you probably have already asked yourself some version of this question. You probably sense— it might be little more than a tingle in your stomach right now—that you're not . . . "normal." That feeling might have come suddenly, in response to a quick moment of eye contact with a crush or a sensation that rose up in your stomach in gym class. Or maybe you've pondered this question for years: Am I queer? How do I *know*?

The answer is: we can't tell you.

Sorry. We know that's not super helpful, right at the start of this whole long identity exploration. And we *really* want to be helpful!

But here's the thing. Most people—queer or not—don't know absolutely who they are and who they will be forever. That's just not the kind of knowledge God gives us. What we do know is that being queer is a process, and that exploring and accepting that process is an essential, and exciting, part of what it *means to be queer*.

It's not that different, in some ways, from a faith journey. Some Christians seem secure in their faith from beginning to end. Others waver, doubt, leave the faith, return, then leave again. Some people are comfortable their whole lives in the church they were raised in. Others find their spiritual well-being outside of traditional church. None of those behaviors are wrong. None are invalidating. If you know, if you don't, it's okay.

The same thing is true about knowing who you are, and knowing whether or not you're queer. It's a journey. And that's okay.

★ THE FIRST THING YOU NEED TO KNOW

No matter what kind of identity questions you're struggling with, it's important for you to know that there's nothing wrong with you. Maybe you can accept this today, maybe not. But keep repeating it now, throughout this book, and throughout your life: there's nothing wrong with you. You are created in the image of God, to be exactly the person you are right now.

Anyone who tells you different—and we mean *anyone*—is wrong.

If you identify as trans, nonbinary, or genderqueer, you or your parents might get a little stuck here, wondering something like: If you are the exact person God created you to be, then why did God give you one body and another gender? On the surface, it may seem weird, impossible, or even a mistake. It isn't. Of course God made trans people trans! God doesn't make mistakes, right?

That may be tough to hear. Especially if the person telling you being queer is wrong is a parent or pastor. Everything inside you may be telling you to stop, telling you to defer to the wisdom of Mom or Pastor Josh. But trust us (we hope we can earn your trust in the course of this book): If anyone—even your parents—says your queerness is a sin, *They. Are. Wrong.* We'll talk more about this later, but we can't repeat it enough. Queer is beautiful, you are beautiful, and anyone who tells you otherwise is wrong. For more, check out *Transforming: The Bible and the Lives of Transgender Christians*, by Austen Hartke.

★ LISTEN TO YOURSELF

It might sound cheesy, but one of the best ways to know who you are is to . . . trust yourself. What does your gut tell you? What are you feeling? Our bodies and emotions are a fundamental part of who we are. They come from God and they are good. God created our ability to feel anger and confusion, happiness and joy. God even created our sexual desire, and our thoughts and feelings about our gender identity. All of our complicated messiness and confusion is part of the image of God in us.

So. Don't hide from your feelings. Do not stifle or deny them. And don't ignore what your body is telling you. If a voice somewhere inside of you is saying you're queer, listen.

And just remember this: Life is long. Questions of identity will surface again and again (and again). You have time to learn who you are. To grow, to change, to declare and redeclare what your queerness is, what your queerness looks like, and what your queerness means to you. Accepting who you are is more important than knowing who you are.

★ LAST THOUGHT

Discovering queerness is always unique, and there is no one easy secret to figuring it out. That's what's so great about it! (And also so frustrating sometimes.) But the discovery process is not an invalidation of who you thought you were. It's a fulfillment of who you are.

Okay. We know this first answer may not have been *that* helpful. But this is where we have to start. It gets clearer from here.

> **David, 24:**
>
> The worst thing about growing up gay in an ultra-conservative Christian environment was the self-hate it insidiously instilled within me—a self-hate which almost tore me apart. Sometimes accepting yourself is the hardest part. When I finally accepted I was gay and was okay with it, it was as if the world came back into color. I can't really describe it otherwise.
>
> And maybe that's why the rainbow is such a powerful symbol. It was like a world, formerly monochrome and dreary, becoming alive once more. While there is no need for labels, accepting myself as gay made

me understand my past experiences: the crushes and the longing for love. It made sense of my past and enabled me to realize that I'm not alone—that there is a community for me.

In that moment, I felt that life, joy, and love were open to me. In a line from my favorite musical, there was "no more need for a heart of stone." Since then, I've come to see God's grace for what it is: free, abundant, and glorious. God loves you. Now start loving yourself.

AREN'T THERE ONLY TWO GENDERS?

Nope!

But we get where this question comes from. Many Christians (and many non-Christians too, of course—this isn't just a Christianity problem) believe there are only two options when it comes to gender: you're either a boy, born with boy parts, or you're a girl, born with girl parts.

The reality is a lot more complex than that!

Every person has a gender identity, and everyone expresses that gender through the manner in which they live.

You, just like literally every person—every adult at church, every kid in every clique in school—have a *gender identity*, an internal sense of who you are. You see yourself in a way no one else can. And how you feel about yourself and your body (including what's between your legs)—that is all part of your gender identity.

Just like every person in the world, you express that gender through the choices you make. That is your *gender expression*. What you wear, how you style your hair, how you walk and talk and dance, even how you sit or move your hands. All the things you do that show the world who you are—that is your gender expression. And that means there are *way* more than two genders. There are an almost infinite number of ways to express gender in the world.

★ TERMS AND CONDITIONS

Let's pause to talk about some terms you might've heard related to gender identity. One term you might've heard is *cisgender*: that refers to people whose gender identity is the same as it was when they were born. Then there's *transgender*: people whose gender identity is different than it was when they were born. Some people also identify as *genderqueer* or

*WORD BREAK: BINARY

Binary means "composed of two things." When it comes to gender and sexuality, we talk about binaries as a way of reducing complicated stuff to two simple options. Anti-queer Christians subscribe to binaries all the time. The gender binary says there are two genders (male and female) and anything else is bad/sinful/icky. Rather than recognize the beauty and wonder of gender diversity, they hold to a strict (and boring!) binary.

nonbinary, which means they don't identify with any of the binary* gender identities, sometimes identifying as both male and female, or as neither.

The rigid rules of the gender binary start right at the moment you're born (pink or blue? dolls or trucks? sports or dance?) and are reinforced *constantly*. You've likely heard it from your parents, or your pastor, or your pals: "Male and female, God created them. How can there be more than two options?" That leads to an important question:

⭐ WHAT IS GENDER?

Well, it's easier to start with what gender is *not*. Gender is not biology. (Did you know that biology is not binary, either? There are actually hundreds of developmental differences in sex conditions that create a wide spectrum of birth assigned sex.) *Man* and *woman* are not genders. Rather, what it *means* to be a "man" or a "woman" (or both, or neither) in the time and place that you live, and in the mind and body God gave you—*that's* gender.

For instance: Do you wear lipstick, tights, and dresses? Those are feminine traits (at this point in time, in many cultures). Do you love sports, or talking trash with your friends? Are you prone to showing off? Masculine. These are *gender norms*, which are all the cultural expectations you feel about how you should look and act. Those norms come from our families, our churches, movies, television, everywhere. They help enforce the binary understanding of gender, but they are nothing more than rules made up by people that change from place to place and generation to generation. There are plenty of boys who like tights and a whole lotta girls who like sports.

All cultures throughout human history teach us that the gender binary is false. From the moment people started making the gender rules, queer folks have been there, writing their own rules.

★ HISTORY!

Did you know that the high-heel shoe was invented in Paris in the seventeenth century as a way for a nobleman to show off his silk-stocking-clad calves? It's true! The high heel was popularized by wealthy men who loved tights and wanted to show off their sexy calf muscles. It was normal, because gender was defined differently in the court of Louis XIV than it is today.

We can even see nonbinary gender expression in the Bible. Eunuchs, as theologian Austen Hartke describes them, were "the gender diverse people of the ancient world" who "lived outside the boundaries of sex and gender." Basically, queer people. Did you know there were queer people in Bible times? Jesus did. And he was like, *It's totally fine, everyone, chill out.* In Matthew, Jesus tells his disciples, "For there are eunuchs who have been so from birth, and there are eunuchs who have been made eunuchs by others, and there are eunuchs who have made themselves eunuchs for the sake of the kingdom of heaven. Let anyone accept this who can" (Matthew 19:12 NRSV). Yeah! JESUS SAID THAT!

Later, in Acts, an angel instructs Philip to join the chariot of an Ethiopian eunuch. Philip does, they read some scripture, and the eunuch asks Philip to baptize them. Philip did *not* say, *Sorry, I can't baptize you because you do not fit in our gender binary.* He just baptized the eunuch immediately, making them one of the very first Christians.

★ LAST THOUGHT

There's never been a time in human history when there were "only two genders." Lots of people do not understand gender nonconforming and transgender identities. That's okay. But that doesn't mean we aren't real.

TWO GENDERQUEER PEOPLE IN HISTORY

1. **EMPEROR ELAGABULS: ROMAN EMPEROR FROM CE 218 TO 222.** In general, it's not a great idea to use today's language for historical people. Still, the emperor Elagabuls was so, so, *so* trans that we're making an exception. From childhood, Elagabuls was known to be living beyond the boundaries of male gender norms and later even sought out gender confirmation surgery. As emperor, Elagabuls offered huge sums of money to any doctor who could "equip him with female genitalia."

2. **JOAN OF ARC: FRENCH HERO BORN 1412. BURNED BY THE CHURCH IN 1431.** Ahh, Joan. Hero, badass, superbly queer. Joan was a soldier who was told by God that she would successfully lead the French armies against the English invasion in the fifteenth century. Which she did. She was then, you may have heard, burned at the stake by the church. There were lots of reasons the church wanted to get rid of Joan, but do you know how they ended up doing it? The charge they were able to convict Joan for? Queerness. That's right. She dressed and acted like a man. Which meant, according to the patriarchal church, that she had to die.

IS THERE SOMETHING WRONG WITH ME?

Absolutely not. Let's move on. . . .

Wait! Why do so many people think there's something wrong with me?

Okay. We hear you. This question might get a little dicey, but we have to get a few things clear here and now. So buckle up.

Every teenager feels shame, embarrassment, confusion. It's a part of growing up and finding out who we are. But not every teenager has adults in their lives telling them they are fundamentally defective. Telling them a core part of their very nature is sinful. Telling them that, if they accept who they are, they will go to hell.

For queer Christians, this is a too-common message, and it is *wrong*.

We don't say this lightly, but it's not just wrong to say these things. It is complete nonsense. It is anti-Christian. You are created exactly as God intended—"fearfully and wonderfully." Anyone who disagrees can take it up with the Psalms. (And they'll lose that argument, because it's in Psalm 139:14).

Still. We know that writing these words is unlikely to win the day against a parent or pastor or teacher who holds anti-LGBTQ+ positions. It might not even win the day against your own self-doubt, fear, shame, or anxiety. Hang on, though. Please.

★ THE NUMBERS

This book isn't going to lie to you. We are always going to give it to you straight (so to speak!). So there's no point in denying that there are a lot of people who are going to think there is something wrong with you.

It's true that LGBTQ+ support has come a long way, very quickly, in the last decade. And a lot of that support is

What does it mean to be affirming? We use this word a lot so it's good to get a clear understanding of what we mean.

An affirming adult or church understands that queerness is part of God's creation. Our queerness is an integral part of how we're made, and it is a cause for celebration. They do not view us as sinful, or expect celibacy, or ever try to change who we are. Rather, they actively support us and advocate on our behalf.

happening in churches, as more and more become open and affirming in their theology and practices when it comes to queer congregants. That is something to celebrate. If you're in such a community, congratulations.

But there remains a lot of work to do.

CHRISTIANS & QUEERNESS

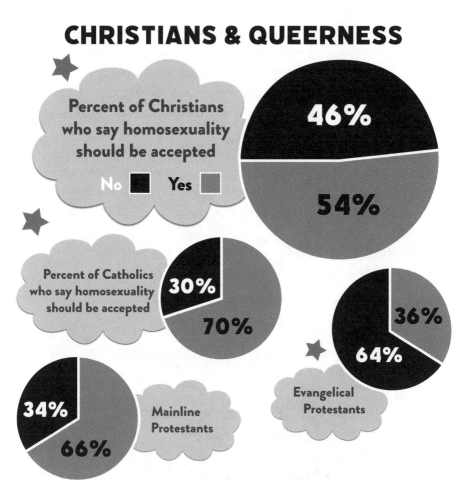

Percent of Christians who say homosexuality should be accepted

No ■ Yes □

46%

54%

Percent of Catholics who say homosexuality should be accepted

30%

70%

36%

64%

Evangelical Protestants

34%

66%

Mainline Protestants

Many Christians reject queerness and queer humanity (of course, no matter what anyone argues, our humanity is not up for debate!).

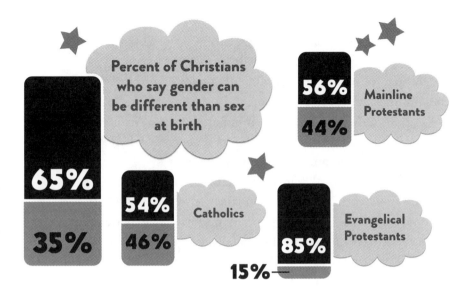

Percent of Christians who say gender can be different than sex at birth

65% / 35%

54% / 46% — Catholics

56% / 44% — Mainline Protestants

85% / 15% — Evangelical Protestants

If you or your family attend a non-affirming church, here are a few things to remember:

* Welcoming faith communities exist, and they're eagerly awaiting your arrival.

* Even in non-affirming churches, there are likely allies. Even a few vocal supporters can make all the difference in our lives!

* Your value comes from God. Not from the people in your church.

The point of this data is not to bum you out. It's meant to educate and prepare you. We know that the only acceptable number for LGBTQ+ acceptance in the church—and everywhere else—is 100 percent. We also know there's a long way to go.

★ ADULTS CAN BE (AND OFTEN ARE) WRONG

Here's a not-so-secret: A lot of people are wrong about a lot of things. And when it comes to the humanity of LGBTQ+

people, there's only one answer we accept: *it's that you are beloved!* Everyone who disagrees is, in fact, incorrect.

Which means it's very possible that a lot of authority figures in your life are wrong about you and your queerness. So here's an important lesson to keep in mind at all times: *Not every adult should be considered an authority figure!* Especially when it comes to *you.* You are the one who knows you best.

When others speak harmfully against your queerness—especially when it's someone you trust—it reinforces what shame, anxiety, or self-doubt you may already be experiencing. It's crucial to be prepared, emotionally and mentally, for how you will protect yourself from such messages.

Here are some general tips for dealing with unsupportive adults:

* You don't have to respond. It's not your job to educate the adults in your life. Sometimes the best thing you can do for yourself is walk away.

* Write or repeat affirmations to yourself every day. Whatever you need to hear. Say it in the mirror. Write it on your hand. Even if you don't believe it yet, keep saying it because it's true.

  Try: I AM BEAUTIFUL.

  GOD LOVES MY QUEERNESS.

  I'M PROUD TO BE (FILL IN THE BLANK).

* Talk to a supportive, affirming counselor or therapist who is not part of your faith community.

Finding safe, supportive people outside of our social and family life to discuss our joys, struggles, and emotions with is one of the most potent tools in the queer toolbelt. The earlier you start, the better. It's not always easy to advocate for good mental health support in all situations, but as much as you are able, try to find a good fit.

* Limit contact with any adult who tells you something is wrong with you. That's not always possible. But when it is, do it.

The sooner you find out how to take care of your emotional, spiritual, and mental well-being, the better equipped you'll be to thrive. Of course, this is all easier said than done, especially if those adults happen to be your parents. We'll talk specifically about parental rejection later, but for now, just know that you are the only authority on who you are.

★ LAST THOUGHT

Because it bears repeating: There is *nothing* wrong with you.

It's difficult to ignore degrading or discriminatory messages about oneself. Implying or stating that "there's something wrong with you" is *definitely* homophobic or transphobic. If you're hearing homo/transphobic messages from your parents or from the pulpit of your church, the teachers in your classroom, and the leaders of your youth group, then you should be prepared, mentally and emotionally, for how you will respond.

And remember, you don't deserve it.

Smith, 31:

This is the question I asked myself the most as a young adult struggling to come to terms with my sexual preference: Is there something wrong with me? Did God make me like this? Was it something I did? Some kind of perversion? Growing up in the Pentecostal tradition, there were many answers to this question—none of them helpful, most of them harmful.

But as I learned to accept who I am, I began to see my attraction to the same gender as something that I couldn't change. I saw that it was a major factor to both my uniqueness and my perspective as an individual. I went through reparative therapy. I went through exorcisms, prayers, lectures, seminars—everything I could think of to change my sexual orientation. But nothing worked. And the more I talked with others who were with me on this journey, the more I realized it didn't work for them, either. That's when I decided to accept being gay as part of who I am as a person.

Here's what I can say now, as an adult struggling with this question. No, there is nothing wrong with me being gay. There never was. I am blessed and thankful that I inhabit a body that allows me to experience "masculinity" and "femininity" and all the colors in between. I was given a gift, and my only regret is that it took me nearly thirty years to fully treasure it.

CAN I BE QUEER AND CHRISTIAN?

Yes. You can be queer and Christian.

God loves you—and that includes your queerness. God loves you not in spite of, but *because of*, who you are. There is no contradiction between being queer and having a relationship with God.

However, just because it is *possible* to be queer and Christian does not mean it is *easy* to be queer and Christian. The sad reality is that—depending on where you live, your family, your religious context, all kinds of things—it can be hard to be a queer Christian. If it's hard for you, we're sorry, and please know it's not because you're queer and it's not because of God, either! It's because of other Christians—Christians who tell you that your queerness is wrong.

If your home environment, church teaching, or faith community is of the kind that claims you cannot, in fact, be queer and Christian at the same time, here are two things to keep in mind:

1) **GOD MADE YOU TO BE EXACTLY WHO YOU ARE.** Your queerness is not an accident or a mistake. The Bible says you are "fearfully and wonderfully made" (Psalm 139:14). Or, as we like to say, you are *queerfully* and wonderfully made—God is the one who made you queer! Let no one convince you otherwise.

1) **ANTI-LGBTQ+ THEOLOGY CAN BE DEADLY.** You don't need to change. But even if you want to, trying to change your sexual orientation or gender identity is *extremely dangerous*. We will discuss more about that later, but for now, please: *Don't try to change yourself*—instead, change your theology. Protecting yourself emotionally and spiritually often means examining what you're taught and what you believe. It's okay to leave a church that teaches bad theology (if it's possible and safe to do so!)

★ THE NUMBERS

There are queer Christians everywhere in the United States, regardless of what you may hear from the people around you. About 41 percent of LGBTQ+ folks in the US say they're Christian, and that's, like, millions of people.*

> ***It's super hard to count LGBTQ+ Americans. But even if we take the lowball number and assume 4.5% of the United States is queer,**

that means there are over 14.7 million queer people in the United States, and the data suggests that nearly half of them are religious. You have company!

But the numbers also testify to the difficulty of being queer and Christian. A 2019 study found that gay and lesbian college students who said "religion is very important to me" were 38 percent *more likely* to have considered suicide than their straight peers.

What this means is that Christians have a harder time accepting their queerness than non-Christians do. This is real and needs to be reckoned with by all people of faith. Wherever you are in your relationship to your church and your queerness, remember, your value comes from God, who loves you and your queerness.

If you're experiencing suicidal thoughts or are thinking of hurting yourself, there is help.

- ★ **National Suicide Prevention Hotline: 1-800-273-8255**
- ★ **Crisis Text Line: Text "HOME" to 741741**
- ★ **Trevor Project LGBTQ+ Support Line: 1-866-488-7386**
- ★ **Trans Lifeline: 1-877-565-8860**

★ SOME WORDS ABOUT LEAVING THE CHURCH

Many LGBTQ+ folks have been hurt, traumatized, or abandoned by their churches and Christian communities. Many don't feel welcome anymore. Some will find affirming congregations later in life, while others may never return to Christianity, instead finding supportive spiritual communities outside of religion. Regardless, a majority of queer people have found—in the church or out—that a fulfilling spiritual life goes hand-in-hand with an authentically lived queer life.

This doesn't mean you have to cultivate any particular spiritual practice or religious belief. It just means that you should not assume your queerness is incompatible with your faith. If you are both queer and Christian, don't run away from that. Your understanding of those words may change over time, but you don't have to sacrifice one part of your identity for the sake of the other.

Finding your way in the world as a queer person of faith can be a beautiful thing. And yes, it can be difficult. If you end up needing to leave your church for a time, regardless of how long you're gone or where you come back to a faith community, that's okay. Others may judge you, but screw 'em. They aren't the ones that decide who you are and what God thinks of you (spoiler: God will love you no matter what). Don't judge yourself for protecting yourself. God won't either.

★ LAST THOUGHT

God wants you to be safe, to recognize your worth, and to love yourself regardless of where you worship or what you believe.

> **Cleo, 28:**
>
> When I sort through all the rhetoric and fear and the handful of verses of Scripture that scared people use as weapons, I still cannot convince myself that God, the God I experience through faith and through the Bible, would want me to apologize for loving anyone. Can you really, truly imagine that someone who sent Jesus to look for the most hated and ostracized people and show them compassion would tell you that you love the wrong type of person? I've heard genuine same-sex love twisted into something ugly and perverse and different, which just isn't

reality. It's no less pure and no different than the love between husbands and wives that you hear celebrated in churches every day.

Love is a human instinct and when it's shoved down for any reason, it does something to you. I didn't realize that until recently. I spent a long, long time convinced that I was fundamentally broken and incapable of giving or accepting love, because my natural impulse to love included other women and [some people thought] that was unacceptable. Coming to terms with my sexuality gave me my ability to love back, and that's what makes me feel close to God.

WHERE DO I FIND ACCURATE INFORMATION?

If you're reading this book, odds are you've already scoured the internet with your most pressing questions about being queer and Christian. We also think the odds are good that you didn't find exactly what you needed—hence, this book. But for the next time you head to the internet for answers to pressing questions, we've got some pointers.

The internet is a big and wonderful place. Sometimes. It can also be *the worst*. We'll talk more about the sometimes-beautiful/sometimes-horror-movie potential of the internet later. For now, we just want to give you a few words of warning when looking for answers online about your queerness, your faith, or your community.

★ WHAT TO KEEP IN MIND ONLINE

A few things to keep in mind when looking for answers to any and all questions about faith, queerness, or any other matters in life:

- Not all statistics and data are reliable (some of it is intentionally unreliable).

- Not all information is helpful (some of it is purposely harmful).

- Target your search ahead of time. Don't just Google a question. Go to a reliable LGBTQ+ resource (see the resource list at the back of this book to get started).

- Everyone has a bias. Some people are better than others at keeping their biases in check, but it's crucial to start recognizing harmful biases.

This last one is so, so, *so* crucial to keep in mind that we're going to repeat it.

- Everyone has a bias.

Many Christians have become very, very good at hiding their queerphobic beliefs. Take a phrase like "all are welcome." It's beautiful. You might hear it every week during communion. "All are welcome" *should* mean what it says: *ALL are welcome.* And at a lot of churches this *is* what it means. But sometimes it's not. Sometimes this phrase is explicitly used to harm LGBTQ+ people, by hiding anti-queerness beliefs in the language of love-the-sinner-hate-the-sin. "All are welcome" can be a truly welcoming statement or a truly awful one used to mask an anti-queer bias.

You will find the same kind of people, language, and hidden biases online. That's why it's so important to do your research. Learn the language of queer-affirming Christianity, and get familiar with online faith communities. Push past generic statements like "All are welcome" and try to find the webpages where churches get specific about what they believe about queer people. If you're not doing your research, you might find yourself—online or IRL—somewhere you thought was helpful but that ends up being very much the opposite.

★ WORD OF ADVICE!

Your well-being depends on accepting your innate value, given to you by God. Do not give your time or mental energy to reading "both sides" when it comes to you living an authentic, whole life. Your queerness is a wonderful and enriching part of you. About that fact there is only one side worth listening to: the one that affirms you exactly as you are.

★ LAST THOUGHT

Know how teachers get grumpy when you use junk websites for research papers? Well, we'd like to remind you that the same principle holds true for your life. If you're asking questions about who you are, wouldn't you want to know that the people who are answering actually know what the heck they're talking about?

Yeah.

IS THIS A PHASE?

Here are four awful words that, in all likelihood, you either have heard or will hear: "It's just a phase." The only thing worse—which you've probably also heard—is "You'll grow out of it." And sure, sometimes we do go through phases (sporty phase, goth phase, skater phase). That's the thing about self-discovery: sometimes you have to try things on to find out what fits. That's just part of being human. There's nothing wrong with going through phases.

But when it comes to your sexual orientation and gender identity, the concept of "going through a phase" should be thrown out entirely. LGBTQ+ identities are not phases.

There are a couple things going on in this question, so let's break it into two parts.

★ PART ONE: IS QUEERNESS EVER A PHASE?

We all go through phases, right? Maybe you were a jock in middle school, but you gave that up for band in high school, and later in college you can start that tortured, brooding intellectual phase. Tempting, then, to think that your queerness is just a phase and you will later return to a straight/cisgender life.

The reality is, queerness is rarely a passing phase. Most people (*not everybody*) in the LGBTQ+ community start having queer feelings or thoughts early in life. We *aren't* talking about coming out here. We're just talking about some sense inside of us. We might ignore it, or maybe we don't even have words to describe it. But usually it's there.

One study showed that feelings of same-sex attraction in lesbian, gay, bi, and pan+ people emerged, on average, at eleven years old. Transgender and gender-nonconforming people often feel a disconnect between their self and their body even earlier in life.

But age doesn't really matter. We are who we are, and we all find ourselves in our own time.

★ PART TWO: ON THE WAY TO GAY

Even if you've accepted that *being queer* is usually not a phase for the vast majority, you may still be asking: Is *my* queer identity just a phase?

This question is *particularly* resonant for bisexual people, whose identities are often demeaned as being "on the way to gay." The idea that bisexuality represents merely "a step" toward accepting that one is gay or lesbian contributes to a problem known as bisexual erasure. Bi erasure questions, or even denies, the existence of bisexual people by assuming that nobody is *really* bisexual. This is nonsense. Harmful nonsense.

Bisexual people are by far the largest group within the LGBTQ+ community. Still, bi erasure is commonplace both inside and outside the queer community. As a result, bisexuals face higher rates of depression and anxiety, and are more likely to participate in risky behavior than lesbian and gay individuals.

However you identify, we can't answer this question for you. All we can tell you is that things change. You might identify one way today, another tomorrow. Some know right away, others take years or decades to find the right label. And still others entirely reject the idea that they need to apply a label. None of this makes your queerness a phase.

★ RED FLAG

When the question "Is this a phase?" comes from the people around us, it can be dangerous. People who think your queerness is a phase may be intending to help you get *out* of that phase. And that road leads to conversion therapy.

In reality, a *tiny* fraction of people who come out "realize" later that they're not LGBTQ+. Many Christians who "reject their queerness" have been manipulated through conversion therapy and will "change back." There is no evidence that conversion therapy works.

Whether this question comes from a place of true concern or is rooted in anti-queer beliefs doesn't matter. Opening the door to the possibility that you might grow out of your LGBTQ+ identity has the potential to do real damage.

★ LAST THOUGHT

A quick final point, because it's helpful to remember: queerness is a journey. Don't be afraid of change. Change is growth. A healthy, vibrant queer identity means making space in your life for change.

Sadie, 21:

Sometimes people go through phases. The problem with calling something a "phase" is how negative its connotations are. There's nothing wrong with going through a "phase," even, and especially, when it comes to your identity.

If something doesn't feel right, never be afraid to say so. Even if it is a "phase," it will never be "just" a phase. I went through phases in high school where I questioned my orientation and gender identity—a result of hating my body and feeling confident in suits. I'm still here, I'm still queer. It's not a phase that I like women, it's not a phase that Elton John likes men. Whatever you're going through, it's likely not a phase either.

There's nothing wrong with being transgender or bisexual or gay or genderqueer or asexual or having any Queer identity. But even if it is a phase, that's perfectly fine. You're still valid, and you're still loved and important.

WON'T PEOPLE THINK I'M DOING THIS FOR ATTENTION?

Coming out as queer just for the attention is a really terrible idea, and there's pretty much no research out there that says that it happens. And there is a good reason that it doesn't happen: Coming out is really, really hard. Coming out has life-changing consequences. We have *lots* to say about coming out later, but for now, as you think about who you are and what lies ahead of you, it's important to realize that your queerness is part of you. It's not something one "does" to "get attention." Seriously. That doesn't even make sense.

★ THEY'RE STILL GOING TO THINK IT

You might be reading this and thinking, "Sure, but even if I'm not looking for attention, after I come out people *will still think I am*."

And you know what? You're right. Some people *are* going to think this. It might be coming from people you really like. Or people who you absolutely can't stand.

At the end of the day, though, it doesn't matter who makes this claim. Hearing it is always frustrating and hurtful. So why do they say it?

★ GASLIGHTING

Straight talk: If anyone says you're queer because you want attention, they're acting like a jerk. Even if it's your best-friend-forever-and-ever, this behavior is, at best, jerky. Sorry to have to say this (we're not really sorry), but the accusation that you just want attention is another way of saying you're lying. It denies that you are the person God made you to be, and it's a cruel form of gaslighting. It should *not* be tolerated. Get away from the gaslighters!

> Gaslighting is when someone tries to make you doubt what you know to be true. If enough voices around you are telling you that you are *not* queer, you might start to believe them instead of yourself. The goal is to make you not trust your own mind, and it is damaging to experience.

Let the gaslighters think what they want. You don't have to defend your existence to anyone. It's not easy to do, but as much as you can, limit your time around people who make the attention-seeking accusation. If they *are* your friend, they'll come to understand who you are and love you for every fabulous fiber of your queer self.

★ PARENTAL MANIPULATION

The attention question is trickier when it's coming from within your home. Avoiding contact with your parents often is not an option. Like the "Is this a phase?" question, accusations of attention-seeking could be coming from a place of concern for you or your safety. And while that may seem understandable, it doesn't make the concern any more valid.

Please, if your parents are unsupportive, remember this: You are a separate human person from your parents (crazy, right?!). They don't know you like you do; they don't get to decide who you are. God decided that, you have accepted it, and if they are going to be part of your future, they'll have to accept it too. (They probably will! But we'll talk more about parental acceptance a little later).

★ LAST THOUGHT

Being queer means being ourselves. We're not "doing" anything but trying to live healthy, whole, authentic, meaningful lives. Attention has nothing to do with anything! When you hear this response, try to remember it's coming from other (usually straight) people, and whatever reason they have for thinking or saying it, it has nothing to do with who you are. Which is a beloved, badass, queer, dear child of God.

> **Anthoni, 28:**
>
> I got this response from a church counselor when I was thirteen. I'd been so nervous to say I liked girls out loud that I had to lean my head back against the wall because I thought I was going to pass out. She promptly assured me I was probably just looking for a sense of identity like anyone my age. She suggested that thinking I was gay because I liked girls was like someone who assumes they have a brain tumor every time they get a headache. Basically, I was overreacting. She said all this with such misguided warmth and reassurance that I believed her.
>
> The attention you get from being queer, especially as someone in a faith community, is hardly desirable. I was about fourteen when Massachusetts became the first state to legalize same-sex marriage. I was very aware of my preference for girls by then, and I heard the vicious national response all around me. I—a kid who loved baking, history books, visiting

my grandpa, and volunteering with friends—heard myself put in the same category as murderers and people who have sex with dogs, heard that I was ruining families, that God wouldn't be able to stand having someone like me around him in heaven. In Sunday school, I heard all about how LGBTQ people were "too loud," "too obnoxious," too everything.

I can't imagine why anyone would ever come out for attention if this was the kind of attention they were going to get.

AREN'T QUEER PEOPLE DISCRIMINATED AGAINST? THAT TERRIFIES ME . . .

Remember that time, earlier, when we said we weren't going to lie to you? Well, we're not. And we're going to level with you right now when we say, yes, queer people do face discrimination. That's why it's important to understand discrimination, what it is, and what you can do if it happens to you.

Legally speaking, explaining what counts as discrimination is actually really tricky. So much depends on what the laws are where you live, or the circumstances in which the discrimination takes place. For example:

* ★ Is bullying discrimination? (Sometimes.)

* ★ What about homophobic harassment? (It depends on who is doing it.)

* ★ Is it illegal to not hire a person because they are queer? (It depends on where you live.)

See? Complicated. Laws are, well, complex.

But laws aren't everything. There is also human decency and

dignity to be considered. Being treated unfairly because of one's queer identity is terrible, always. Even if it's not technically against the law, discrimination is discrimination, no matter what the courts say, and you don't deserve it. Let's set the law books aside and talk about what *you* need to know when it comes to being queer and being treated unfairly.

★ WHAT IS DISCRIMINATION?

discrimination: noun

The practice of treating someone or a group of people less fairly than others.[1]

Fair treatment is good. Unfair treatment is bad. That's pretty obvious, maybe. This is America, after all! Treating everyone fairly, no matter who they are—well, that's sort of America's whole deal.

Our federal government (the one in Washington, DC) has passed laws protecting people against discrimination in school and work on the basis of race, color, religion, sex, and national origin. Those laws are important and necessary.

But. You probably noticed what's missing from that list. It's tragic, but it's true: as of right now, there are no federal protections for LGBTQ+ people in this country. Which means it is *legal* to treat queer people unfairly in this country.

★ REMEMBER, THOUGH, IT'S COMPLICATED

When we say it's legal to discriminate, we have to once again say that we don't mean *everywhere*. Legal protections for queer people in the US are, for now, coming from state governments. Which means it may or may not be legal to discriminate against queer people in your state. It just depends on where you live.

---

1   All definitions are from *Oxford Learner's Dictionary,* unless otherwise noted.

Twenty-one states, plus Washington, DC, have passed laws protecting people from workplace discrimination based on sexual orientation and gender identity.

That's not enough, we know. And unfortunately, the situation in schools is even worse. Only thirteen states—and, again Washington, DC—have passed laws protecting students from discrimination in schools.

These realities are dispiriting, but they are only one small part of the legal situation in any given place. Try not to get discouraged—lots of queer people have been where you are, no matter *where* you are.

★ WHAT SHOULD YOU DO?

The numbers on discrimination toward queer people aren't great, and we're not going to dwell on them. Being treated unfairly sucks. Whether discrimination is legal or not, whether it is intentional or not, is irrelevant. Any rule or policy or behavior that treats LGBTQ+ people differently *is discrimination.* If we could wave a magic wand and erase all of it from the planet, we'd do it. Because we love you. But we can't.

There are a few things to remember, though.

1) **Discrimination is not unique to queer people.**
   There are plenty of racists, misogynists, and bigots in the world. Of course, discrimination being common doesn't make it okay (it's *never* okay!). But it does mean that discrimination is probably something you will experience as a queer person. If you are a person of color, disabled, or belong to any other minority group, discrimination is likely to be even worse (we are so sorry).

Vocab lesson: the reality of an individual of being discriminated against due to multiple traits is called **intersectionality**. The term *intersectionality* was coined by Kimberlé Crenshaw, a lawyer and professor whose work on race theory has changed the way many see the world. Intersectionality is a way of understanding that discrimination multiplies based on one's identity. Whether one is disabled, a person of color, living in poverty, or part of another minority, adding queerness to that identity can compound the amount and impact of discrimination, violence, or oppression. When looking for a counselor or therapist, it's important to find someone who understands the dynamics of all of your identities.

2) Discrimination isn't your fault.

The truth is, anti-queer discrimination is everywhere. In a recent study, 71 percent of LGBTQ+ youth reported experiencing discrimination due to their sexual orientation or gender identity. That's a lot.

It's horrible and it is never, ever, *ever* your fault. The fact that individuals, faith communities, and laws discriminate against LGBTQ+ people is unrelated to your queerness. As always, try to limit your exposure to those people and places with a history of discrimination.

3) Do your research.

It's isolating when the world treats you unfairly. We know, because we've felt it too. Keep in mind, though, that others have gone before you. You are not alone in your experience of being discriminated against, even if you feel alone right now. And those who have come before you are trying to help, by creating the resources we need. Look online for safe, friendly places to go in your town or area. Is there a coffee shop known for being an LGBTQ+ haven? Or a bookstore with a queer-friendly book club? See if your city or state has an LGBTQ+ Chamber of Commerce that lists businesses that are explicitly queer-owned or queer-affirming. These places can be safe havens from discrimination, or resources to fight back against discrimination.

If you're in a rural area or don't have physical access to affirming spaces, online communities like trevorspace.org or empyclosets.com can provide crucial support.

★ LAST THOUGHT

Discrimination is a society-wide issue that we all face. We can't make it disappear, but we can remind you, again, that we're sorry, it's not your fault, and you do not deserve it. And remember, our community is full of advocates and activists fighting back against a culture of discrimination to make your experience, and the experience of those coming out after you, better.

HOW DO I COPE WITH ANXIETY AND DEPRESSION?

Listen up. If you don't need this one, go ahead and skip it. Not all queer people struggle with mental health issues like anxiety and depression. And if you don't, congratulations. You're one of the lucky few—because it's simply a fact that many queer-identifying people, and queer Christians in particular, struggle with anxiety and depression.

For those of us who face this challenge, it is something we have to address. We'll be honest with you, and you must, *must*, MUST be honest with yourself.

★ FIRST AND FOREMOST

The reason that queer people—especially queer teens, and *double especially* queer Christian teens—are more likely to struggle with anxiety and depression is *not* because we are queer. Feelings of sadness, isolation, and fear are part of the human experience. They are part of being a young person. And an adult. These feelings are not a sign that anything is wrong with you.

You are *not* the problem.

Being queer is not the problem.

★ SOME TOUGH NUMBERS

Still. There's no denying that rates of anxiety and depression are higher in the queer community than among non-queer folks.

"DEPRESSED MOST OR ALL OF THE TIME"

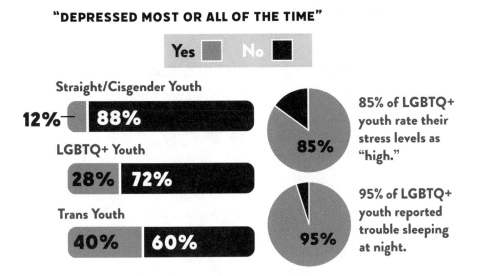

Yes ▇ No ▇

Straight/Cisgender Youth
12% — 88%

LGBTQ+ Youth
28% 72%

Trans Youth
40% 60%

85% of LGBTQ+ youth rate their stress levels as "high."

95% of LGBTQ+ youth reported trouble sleeping at night.

We also know that higher rates of anxiety and depression mean queer teens are engaging in more risky behavior than their straight peers. When it comes to drinking, taking drugs, and having unsafe sex, we are struggling. Studies show that LGBTQ+ youth are more likely to engage in risky health-related behaviors.

This is the upsetting and dangerous reality of too many queer young people. BUT. We also know that these numbers are directly linked to *family acceptance*. Queer teens who are accepted and affirmed by their parents are no more likely than straight teens to face these issues.

That points to some of the causes for anxiety and depression for queer people. Depression and anxiety have many causes, including genetic predisposition, chemical imbalances in the brain, and, most crucially for queer people, life circumstances:

the level of acceptance vs. rejection you might face in your everyday life. Not on the list of causes for anxiety and depression, though? Being queer. We said this already, but it's worth saying again: Blaming your queerness might be easy when you feel low. But your queerness is a beautiful part of you that deserves celebration, not stigma.

★ CHRISTIANITY AND QUEERNESS

For many, there's an additional psychological burden that comes with being queer and Christian. Depending on your church teaching and congregation, the reality can be that your faith communities are, very often, making the lives of queer people harder.

In fact, research on religion and sexual orientation shows that people who are either lesbian, gay, bisexual, or questioning and are "very religious" are more likely to struggle with suicidal thoughts than those who are straight and religious.

Yeah. We know. That is messed up. But it's not that hard to imagine, right? The love of God is in us, and we are all beloved children of our Maker. But too often, the Christians around us do not extend their love to all parts of who we are. And that hurts. It creates shame. It isolates us from the people around us. And it can lead us to scary places.

Please know that whatever you're feeling, whether it's joyful or proud, or anxious and jumpy, or alone and depressed, it's normal. Don't judge yourself. Feel your feelings. But if you think you need help, ask for it.

If you're experiencing suicidal thoughts or are thinking of hurting yourself, there is help.

- ★ **National Suicide Prevention Hotline: 1-800-273-8255**
- ★ **Crisis Text Line: Text "HOME" to 741741**

- ★ **Trevor Project LGBTQ+ Support Line:** 1-866-488-7386
- ★ **Trans Lifeline:** 1-877-565-8860

★ WHAT YOU CAN DO

1) BE HONEST WITH YOURSELF.

If your feelings are overwhelming, acknowledge them. Denying how you feel, avoiding the challenges that you face, will only create more work for you later.

2) EDUCATE YOURSELF.

Knowledge is power. It's a cliché, but sometimes the clichés have some truth in them. Learning about mental health is step one in recognizing, coping, and living with mental-health issues. We'll start with some definitions and signs of anxiety and depression.

anxiety: noun

Feeling nervous or worried that something bad is going to happen.

Anxiety is a normal part of life. Everyone experiences it. But feelings of overwhelming worry or panic may require professional attention. Here are some symptoms of anxiety to look out for:

- ✴ Feeling nervous or restless
- ★ Fast heart rate and/or rapid breathing
- ★ Sweating and/or trembling
- ★ Feeling weak or tired
- ★ Trouble concentrating on anything other than the thing you are worried about
- ✴ Trouble sleeping

depression: noun

> 1. A medical condition in which a person feels very sad and anxious and often has physical symptoms such as being unable to sleep.
> 2. The state of feeling very sad and without hope.

Depression is different than anxiety, though often the words are used together. And while anxiety can be a symptom of depression, it's important to understand them both separately. Depression is characterized, generally, as persistent and consistent feelings of sadness and/or hopelessness. Here are some symptoms of depression to look out for:

* Feelings of sadness, emptiness, and/or hopelessness
* Angry outbursts and frustrations, even over minor issues
* Loss of interest or pleasure in normal activities like hobbies or sports
* Difficulty sleeping and/or too much sleep
* Lack of energy
* Changes in diet, including lack of appetite or overeating
* Self-harm
* Poor performance or attendance in school
* Feeling misunderstood and extremely sensitive
* Using recreational drugs and/or alcohol

3) GET HELP IF YOU NEED IT.

Anxiety and depression are not signs of weakness. They are common conditions that can come in short-term bouts or stay for the long haul, but when treated, are completely manageable.

Ask yourself: If you were having problems falling asleep at night and perhaps trouble breathing, and you went to the doctor and the doctor said, "You have a bronchial infection," what would you do? You would treat the infection, right?

Now ask yourself: If you were having problems sleeping at night, maybe breaking out in sweats and unable to focus your mind long enough to actually fall asleep, what would you do?

Too many queer teens are doing nothing about this. Please don't be one of them.

Talk to a doctor. Talk to a therapist. There's no shame in having a bronchial infection. And there's no shame in having anxiety or depression. These are common and treatable.

4) DON'T JUDGE YOURSELF.

Love yourself.

⭐ LAST THOUGHT

This one's for everyone, whatever your relationship to your mental health: Take a deep breath and remember that God loves you. Whatever your present situation is, your future looks good.

> I know the plans I have for you, says the LORD,
> plans for your welfare and not for harm, to give
> you a future with hope.
> —Jeremiah 29:11 NRSV

Michelle, 28:

I first developed depression at about twelve years old. I didn't really know what to do about it. I had all of these confusing feelings, and puberty was hard enough without being bisexual. I loved God, and all I wanted was to be able to be with him and live in peace. All I received from the pulpit was that God thought I was an abomination. Imagine that. A child being led to believe they were a disgusting abomination that deserved to be in hell just for thinking another girl was pretty. I started scratching my upper thigh with a broken piece of plastic. The pain distracted me from all of the feelings and confusion. It became the only way that I could feel anything after becoming so numb to the outside world.

As I got older, it just got worse. I didn't have anyone to talk to, no adult to tell me that who I was was in fact okay, and that I was loved no matter what my sexuality is. The only place I could go to feel free were gay bars, and that turned to an unhealthy lifestyle of drinking (too much), sleeping around (too much), and hard drug use. It was rough because I wanted to reach out to God and worship, but I felt like God hated everything about me. That is all anyone ever told me growing up.

After a few falls to rock bottom, I went begrudgingly back to the church. What I found was nothing short of a miracle. I was free to worship again knowing what I know now. Even though the depression is still there, it's a lot less stressful nowadays. I found people I could talk with, and that lifted the anxiety. I found others just like me.

INTERLUDE:
QUEER CLICHÉS
AND WHAT THEY TEACH US

Clichés are, for the most part, nonsense. They are simplistic and reductive. People—all of us—are complex and filled with layers upon layers upon layers. Clichés, like stereotypes, don't define anyone, ever.

But. You know. Still. And since you're very likely to encounter stereotypes of queer people, built on clichés that have only a teeny little toe in the truth, it's a good idea to know some of them. And then ignore them. Really. Nothing to see here.

1. **GBFs are BFFs.**
   The implication is that GBFs (gay best friends) are the best best friends a girl (usually) can have. This trope is done to death in TV and movies. Friends are friends, gay or not.

2. **All we think about is sex!**
   Well, maybe . . . but how exactly is this a queer-specific problem? Also. It's just not true. Some folks think about sex all the time; others, never; most of us, sometimes. Shrug emoji.

3 & 4. Bisexuals are sex-crazed, promiscuous hounds and/or maybe they don't actually exist?

Okay, so this is really two clichés, but they are related to the same principle: biphobia. Our culture has a really, *really* hard time believing that bisexual people are . . . actually bisexual. It seems like the most complicated bisexual concept the world can handle is "SEX-CRAZED MANIAC" or "on the way to gay," with nothing in between.

Which is insulting and factually incorrect. There are so many bisexual people. *So. Many.* Way more than lesbian or gay folks. Actually, there are about as many bi people as the other two COMBINED! And guess what? They're not all bi in the same way.

5. Lesbians hate men.

As a rule? No.

But it's true that lesbians are not *attracted* to men, and it's also true that our culture—being built on centuries of patriarchy—values men over women. So, maybe the slingers of this cliché are mistaking not "liking" men for not *liking* men.

Whatever it is, get over it. Lesbians rule.

6. Trans people are just confused and will grow out of their gender confusion.

Wait, we're confused? About what? (Spoiler alert: Nothing). You're confused, maybe, but we're just living our lives.

Don't: Be a condescending prick.

Do: Support trans people.

7. Queer folks have excellent GAYDAR.

Gaydar, if you're unfamiliar, is one's ability to *just know* that a person is queer when you see them. Some people say they just have incredible gaydar (and some studies show that gaydar does, in fact, exist!). But gaydar is also used to reinforce stereotypes about queer people, since it assumes that being LGBTQ+ "looks like" something immediately recognizable.

Anyway. Some people have it. Some people don't. (Most don't.)

8. All queer people love astrology.

As a Gemini, I'm offended that anyone would believe that a single trait can define all of our people.

9. You are part of the gay agenda.

Well. Some clichés are true, we suppose. Welcome to the team.

I THINK I'M READY TO TELL SOMEONE. BUT WHO SHOULD I COME OUT TO FIRST?

It's time to talk about coming out. We're going to go in a lot of different directions in the next couple chapters—coming out at home, school, church, the joys and consequences of doing it (or not doing it). But before we get to all that, there are two things we have to tell you right up front:

1. **YOU DON'T *HAVE* TO COME OUT.** Really. Especially if you're not yet sure about your own identity, or don't know who will support you. If you aren't ready to be *that person*, or just plain don't want to, then don't! There's simply no right way or right time to come out as an LGBTQ+ person. Everyone can, and should, do it on their own time, when they're ready. So if you're not, don't sweat it.

2. **IF YOU'RE GOING TO COME OUT, HAVE A PLAN.** Whether you are ready at this very second or are waiting for the right time,

having a thoughtful plan that puts your safety and security first is so, so, *so* important. You'll never regret being prepared.

Remember. You own this process. You don't owe anyone anything. Until the day you choose otherwise, these matters are between you and God.

★ THE NUMBERS ON COMING OUT

If you're ready to come out, congratulations! Coming out is a big deal. It's a major milestone for many queer folks. It's the before-and-after moment that very well might change everything. (Or it might not! We can't tell the future!) But if you're ready to tell someone, that means you've come a long way toward self-acceptance and self-love. And that's good. So we'll say it again: Congratulations!

Every coming-out story is a little bit different, and it can be helpful to have a few points of reference for your own decisions about coming out.

AVERAGE AGE REALIZED LGBTQ+ / CAME OUT

Baby Boomers: Realized 20 / Came Out 23

| 16 | 17 | 18 | 19 | **20** | 21 | 22 | **23** |

Generation X: Realized 18 / Came Out 23

| 16 | 17 | **18** | 19 | 20 | 21 | 22 | **23** |

Millennials: Realized 16 / Came Out 18

| **16** | 17 | **18** | 19 | 20 | 21 | 22 | 23 |

WHO ARE LGBTQ+ MOST LIKELY TO TELL FIRST?

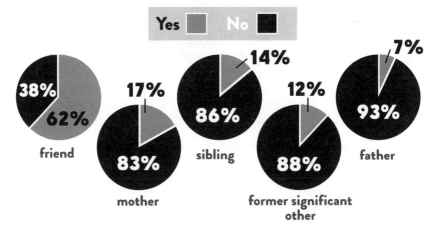

Yes ■ No ■

38% 62%
friend

17%
83%
mother

14%
86%
sibling

12%
88%
former significant other

7%
93%
father

The above numbers are averages across queer communities, so please know that they are not by any means rules we suggest you follow. Honestly, there are no rules. We all just have to feel things out for ourselves. Coming out depends so much upon your individual circumstances that it's really, *really* hard to draw any lines from data to people.

But. We can make two safe assumptions about this data:

1) **QUEER FOLKS ARE COMING OUT EARLIER AND EARLIER**, a trend that points toward greater LGBTQ+ acceptance in the United States.

1) **FRIENDS ARE OFTEN SAFER THAN FAMILY TO TELL FIRST.** Finding a comfortable person to tell is hard, and it's often—though not always—a good idea to start outside your home.

★ MAKING A PLAN

Coming out is not a one-and-done moment. It's a process that you will undergo many times in your life (at school, in college, at work, to your doctor, to your barista, etc.). We're going to do our best to equip you on the many journeys out of the closet that will happen throughout your life. But to do that, we have to start with the very first time you come out.

So, how should you do it? Ultimately that's up to you. But here's a simple four-step plan you can use, adapt, or disregard as you see fit.

1) **MAKE A LIST OF PEOPLE YOU WOULD CONSIDER TELLING.** Make it on paper. Yes. We're asking you to use your hands to write on paper. It's old-fashioned, but it helps to actually write things down. The people on the list should have the qualities that deserve such an honor: loving, trustworthy, gracious, honest, patient, accepting.

2) **CHOOSE A NAME FROM THAT LIST.** Whoever you choose should be someone you are confident will be supportive and will keep the information to themselves. It's very possible you already know who it is. You've thought about it long and hard at this point. Be discerning in your choice, but don't get stuck second-guessing yourself. Circle that person's name, and then thank God that you have such a person in your life.

3) **HAVE THE CONVERSATION.** Find a quiet place to talk, somewhere you're sure you won't be interrupted. Then, tell them as directly as possible. Confide, and be honest. You don't have to have all the answers, and you can answer any questions that come with "I don't know." The important thing at this point is to share.

4) **ASK FOR WHAT YOU NEED.** Whether you are asking for this information to be confidential or asking for support or advocacy in the coming months or years, allow your supporters to do just that: support you.

5) CELEBRATE TOGETHER. You are a beautiful, wonderful, blessed child of God, and you are queer. That is a triumph! CONGRATULATIONS!

You've got a long process in front of you, but you cleared one of the most important hurdles in living an authentic queer life: You came out for the very first time.

> **Emily, 22:**
>
> I first came out to my best friend. I was literally sitting in a Catholic mass and she was sitting in front of me and I just couldn't take it anymore, someone needed to know. I walked up to her after mass and she could tell I was about to cry and I asked her to talk. I basically said, "I'm not straight. And I don't know what I am, but I'm scared of losing everything and I just needed someone else to know."
>
> Over that first year, she was INCREDIBLE. I honestly can't thank her enough. She told me that she loved me and that she was there for me and that she

supported me no matter what. She answered so many crying phone calls that year, helped me sort through my anxieties and feelings, and kept my secret when I asked her to. I know not everyone has this first experience, so I feel very blessed.

I chose to come out to her because I trusted her, because I knew that she wouldn't respond with hate or judgment, but with love. We'd already gone through so much together, and she'd always been there for me, always been a great listener, always been a great friend.

SHOULD I COME OUT TO MY PARENTS/ GUARDIANS? DO I HAVE TO?

Parents.

Of all the coming-out moments in a queer life, few are more worrying than telling your parents. Even if you think they're going to be supportive, it's still a big deal to tell your parents you are queer.

And for Christians, this can be extra complicated. You know why. It's right there in the commandments: "Honor your father and mother." How do we honor our parents by telling them we're queer? Especially if our parents believe that being queer is a sin?

We all ask ourselves at some point: Should I tell them at all?

The reality is: A *lot* of queer people do not come out to their parents in their middle or high school years. And many LGBTQ+ people wait until they no longer live at home to share the news. The average age of coming out to parents is nineteen—the year after many people leave home. A little distance can go a long way.

There are, like, lots and lots of reasons to wait. Sometimes it's necessary—especially if coming out can pose a threat to your safety and security. Or you might just not be ready, or might still be processing your own identity, or might be working through some shame or guilt.

And some Christians may truly not *want* to be LGBTQ+, and are praying for queer thoughts and feelings to just go away. (If this is you, take a look at the chapter about whether or not queerness can be a phase, then come back.)

No matter the reason, the point is that coming out to parents for the first time can truly be terrifying! If it's terrifying to you, you're not alone.

★ THE NUMBERS

There's been a whole bunch of research done on coming out to parents, but not a lot done on coming out to parents *as a Christian*. So we can't tell you *specifically* what to expect.

Here's what we do know:

WHO'S OUT?

LGBTQ+ youth out to parents:
68% are out to their parents about their sexual orientation.
51% are out to their parents about their gender identity.

WHAT DO WE HEAR OUR PARENTS SAY?

78% of youth who are not out to their parents hear negative comments about LGBTQ+ people from their parents.

48% of youth who are out to their parents hear negative comments about LGBTQ+ people from their parents, and are made to feel bad about their own queer identity.

Does it matter if they accept us?
Parental rejection is strongly linked to increased rates of depression; homelessness; suicidal thoughts; drug, tobacco and alcohol use; and other risk factors.

Parental acceptance is strongly linked to greater self-esteem; social support; and lower rates of depression, suicidal thoughts, and substance abuse.

WHAT ABOUT THE "CHRISTIAN" PART?

Christian acceptance of same-sex attraction:

Catholic – 70%	Historically Black
Mainline Protestant – 66%	Protestant – 51%
Orthodox Christian – 62%	Evangelical Protestant – 36%

Christian acceptance of gender can be different from birth sex:

Catholic – 46%	Historically Black
Mainline Protestant – 44%	Protestant – 35%
	Evangelical Protestant – 15%

So what do we learn from all this data?

Most teens do come out to their parents, despite the fact that half of them will hear negative comments directly from their parents (our community is so courageous!).

Whether parents accept or reject queerness has significant and lasting impact on the well-being of their child.

Telling your parents is complicated and risky, and you have to be very careful and discerning about whether and when you want to tell them.

Acceptance of same-sex attraction and gender diversity is improving across Christianity. But "acceptance of same-sex attraction" and that gender diversity exists is not necessarily the same as accepting a queer child in the home.

★ THE RISK, THE REWARD

Ultimately, deciding whether or not to come out to your parents is all about the risks of coming out vs. the possible rewards of coming out. We'll make the list as simple as possible for this one:

> **RISK:** If your parents are not supportive of your queerness, telling them while you are still living in their home can be dangerous physically, emotionally, and/or spiritually. It could even be life-threatening, if they encourage or force you to participate in conversion therapy or force you out of the home.

> **REWARD:** If your parents are supportive of your queerness, telling them is one of the most valuable things you can do to create a healthy and safe future.

These are some mega-sized *ifs*. It's no small thing to consider coming out at home.

⭐ MAKE A PLAN (AGAIN)

Based on the numbers above, lots of you *are* going to come out to parents. Whatever happens afterward, let us be the first to say: Congratulations!! This tells us that you are brave and that you value your queerness. You want to be seen for who you are, and that's worthy of celebrating.

> Everything created by God is good, and nothing is to be rejected, provided it is received with thanksgiving.
> —1 Timothy 4:4 NRSV

For some, coming out at home will be a relief. You'll have it over with, and your parents will express their support. For others, though, coming out *may not* actually feel like a celebratory act. We get that. We know it's hard. Let us celebrate for you, while you make your plan.

PLANNING CHECKLIST FOR COMING OUT TO MOM AND DAD:

☐ **KNOW WHAT YOU WANT TO SAY.** You should be able to say what you are coming out as, and what it means (especially if it is anything other than gay or lesbian).

You should be able to say what this means for your faith. Here are some things you can think about saying, depending on what feels most meaningful for you: *God doesn't make mistakes. God loves me. I am made in the image of God. I am exactly who I was created to be.*

☐ **TALK TO YOUR FRIENDS AND SUPPORTERS.** They can support you, encourage you, and help you figure out how to say what you want to say. And if it doesn't go well, they can comfort you.

If you have already come out in other contexts, do a practice run with a friend or a trusted adult in the role of your parents. Practicing out loud can be really helpful in figuring out what you want to say, and anticipating how your parents will hear it.

- [ ] **PICK A TIME TO HAVE THE CONVERSATION.** Be deliberate about this. Make sure you have some time set aside to process together. Avoid first thing in the morning, right after work, or other times when stress or exhaustion could be a factor for your parents.

- [ ] **HAVE A BACKUP PLACE TO SLEEP ELSEWHERE FOR A NIGHT OR TWO.** Whether you think you'll need it or not, be prepared, and don't make assumptions. Whatever your parents' response, a little space could do you and them some good.

- [ ] **ANSWER THIS QUESTION WITH 100% HONESTY:** Are my parents likely to encourage or force me to attend conversion therapy of any kind, including pray-the-gay-away meetings or change therapy?

  If you even suspect the answer is yes, don't come out. Wait until you are out of the house to tell them (or longer). Your well-being is more important than telling your parents. You don't owe them anything, and conversion therapy DOES NOT WORK.

★ INITIAL REACTIONS

Coming out to our families is a major milestone in the queer journey. But keep in mind that this is a significant time for your parents, too. Things are changing for them, and the future they have imagined for their child will look different.

That's a big deal! It'll take time.

Before you come out to your parents, spend some time preparing yourself for their initial reaction. Whatever response you *think* your family will have, it's best if you prepare yourself for the worst. For some, this prep work will feel unnecessary. Those of you who feel

True, it's a big deal that you do not *have* to worry about right now, but it is worth a mention that our parents are human beings who want to see us succeed, and what that success looks like will be changed by us coming out. Put this in the back of your head and come back to it in ten years. Until then, we're here to help you.

highly confident that you will immediately be showered with love and support by your parents, we are so, so happy for you.

But honestly? That's just not the case for most queer people. Many folks, at least in those crucial first reactions, will get something else. Shock, disbelief, confusion, disappointment, anger—a lot of first reactions are possible, and many of them will feel negative. That negativity might pass in moments—just a brief look on your mom's face, perhaps—or it could last days or, unfortunately, the rest of your life.

That's unlikely. But we mean it: Be prepared for anything.

A lot of what parents hear and how they react when their kids come out stems from a very primal fear: they believe that your life will be harder because you are queer. They are not just thinking about you now. They're thinking about the whole world and what everyone you'll ever encounter for the rest of your life is going to think about their child. That's how parents' minds work. That fear often exists because our parents love us and want us to be safe.

But that fear can be expressed in some very ugly, hurtful, or damaging ways. Common negative responses include:

✴ "Are you sure?" (You wouldn't be coming out if you weren't.)

✴ "This is just a phase." (Probably not.)

✴ "You'll grow out of it." (Highly unlikely.)

✴ "Being gay is wrong." (It isn't.)

✴ "Transgender people are mentally ill." (Nope.)

✴ "Why are you doing this to us?" (It's about you, not them.)

✴ "What did we do wrong?" (Nothing. God made me, queerfully and wonderfully.)

✴ "We are going to fix this!" (Nothing is broken.)

✴ "You can't live under our roof if you are _____!" (Okay. There's no snappy response to this one. It's dangerous and far too common. If you're being threatened with getting kicked out or are actually kicked out, go to "Additional Resources" at the back of this book, find "If you're at risk of homelessness," and get help.)

These responses come from a lot of places: fear, shame, guilt, anger, bad theology, closed-mindedness, lack of education. What they do not represent is you or your queerness.

These responses are about your parents and their issues, not about you.

We're going to repeat that. *It. Is. Not. About. You.*

The good thing about our parents' initial reaction is that (usually) it will not last. You've had a long time to process who you are and what it means. You've built up the courage to come out and have faced some fear and uncertainty about what it all means. But your parents? They haven't. When your parents hear it for the first time, they are truly hearing it for the first time.

They'll have time to consider what it means to have a queer child, and in all likelihood they will come around to love, support, and affirm your beautiful queer life. Research suggests that most parents—over the coming months or years—will become more supporting of their queer child.

You should not put your parents' feelings before your own (unless it's a matter of your safety). But it doesn't hurt to remember that it will take time for your parents to process your queer identity.

★ LAST THOUGHT

Things are going to be different after you come out. Relationships will change. Expectations for your future will change. Lots of things are going to change. But never forget what you've earned: the ability to be your authentic self. Yes, the situation could be tense, even hostile. But take heart. You have done something powerful in honoring yourself—and the one who made you—by announcing who you are to your family.

Whatever happens, be proud of yourself. Know that God loves you, and that your future is in your hands, not your parents'.

Marie, 28:

> I anticipated family disapproval before I came out. To get ahead of the game I made sure that I was in a place mentally/emotionally to come out without being totally crushed when I encountered disapproval. I had to be ready to face it. Otherwise, I wouldn't have been ready to come out. I got to the point where it was worth the trade-off. Being able to be myself is worth any disapproval I face.

WHAT IF MY FAMILY DISAPPROVES?

Rejection is terrible.

Every person everywhere would probably agree: it feels terrible to be rejected. It doesn't matter what kind of rejection it is, either. Being dumped. Not getting the job. Getting cut from the cast of your school's production of *Mamma Mia*. It always feels like, well—it feels like crap.

But there's a special kind of terrible reserved for family rejection. Being on the outs with our own parents is just . . . the . . . WORST.

At least, that's probably how it feels at this very important moment. If you've just come out and you're now facing the disapproval of your family, that can be devastating. And we're sorry if you're in that position. You may be feeling that this can never be repaired. That it'll never get better. But the thing is, what you are feeling is totally normal.

★ IT TAKES TIME

After you come out, your relationship to your family might feel strained and distant. Maybe even hostile. There could be anger, or silence, or sadness. Of course, there could be joy, welcoming love, and celebration, too—congratulations to those of you who are immediately shown love and acceptance!

For the rest of you, here is something you might want to keep in mind: What your parents thought they knew is no longer true, and that can send a shock into every corner of the home. We said it earlier, but they need time. Same with siblings, grandparents, and family friends. Change is hard, and finding out you didn't know what you thought you knew about someone close to you is disorienting.

Research in this subject area shows that regardless of a parent or family's initial reaction to the news that their child is LGBTQ+, parents generally become more accepting of their child over time.

Remember: You've been processing this for a while. They just started.

★ NOT ALL DISAPPROVAL IS EQUAL

So, listen up, please, because this is important. Sometimes families disapprove, and sometimes families *DISAPPROVE*. And it's important to grasp the difference.

If your parents don't accept your queerness and they have expressed that in invalidating ways, that is a frustrating and difficult experience. In those times, remember that you are queerfully and wonderfully made by a God who loves you. Validate yourself among supportive friends, and to the best you are able, hunker down until graduation. This usually works fine as a strategy to keep one safe and on a pathway to a healthy future.

However, if your parents' attitude toward you goes *beyond* regular levels of parental disapproval—for instance, if they disapprove of you so much that you feel like you might be in danger at home, or that you might be kicked out of your home if you stay—please find safety.

You don't have to stay in a dangerous home environment.

Explore staying with a friend or family member if short-term separation might help. If more urgent or permanent actions are necessary, there is help. Reach out to . . .

★ a teacher, guidance counselor, or trusted school administrator.

★ your local LBGTQ+ center.

★ an affirming church (if yours is not, see if there is another in your city or town).

★ LGBTQ+ support hotlines or organizations online.

There are resources in the back of this book that will give you more specific details on finding this help, as well as direction on what to do if you are facing homelessness or need to talk to a counselor or therapist.

Nic, 20:

Here's the thing: Depending on your denomination, a part of your family might very well reject you when you come out. It's awful. And it's also not your fault. The Bible is very clear on loving one another and not judging other people, for God is the only one who can judge us. Sadly, some people don't see it that way yet. But many people do, and they are out there, most likely even within your family, and they can help you find a place where you belong in the world.

My parents don't accept that I am transgender, for now. It hurts me very deeply that they don't. I bring it up every once in a while, hoping they'll change their minds, but in the past three years since I've come out to them, I haven't had any luck. I might never convince them. But I have convinced my sister, who now supports me through everything, and I have a wonderful boyfriend who supports me too. There are people out there for you, and they might not be in your immediate family right now, but the great thing is that you can make your own family out of the people that do support you.

THEY'RE NOT ACCEPTING, BUT THEY LOVE ME. DON'T MY PARENTS KNOW WHAT'S BEST FOR ME?

If your parents do not accept you *and* your queerness, then they do not know what's best for you. They just don't. Even if they love you, even if they're praying for you. Even if they're being advised by the pastor at your family church. It doesn't matter. Just because they love you *does not* mean they know what is best for you.

Alexandra, 29:
> People who care for you sometimes think they know the best way to move forward. Often it is the people who love us, or say they do, who can cause the most damage. The hardest thing for me has been learning to trust myself rather than to discount my experiences when others disagree.

SHOULD I COME OUT AT SCHOOL? (GULP!)

We've talked a bit about your first time coming out, and about telling your parents. If you have started the coming-out process, congratulations! It's a big milestone, and you should celebrate. And if you haven't, wonderful! There's no rush, no pressure. Do it when you're ready. But now it's time to talk about coming out in the wider world.

So. Let's start with school. First thing to do when thinking about being out at school is (you guessed it): make a plan.

★ PROS AND CONS

A great place to start on your coming-out plan for school is a list of pros and cons (these are great for everything, really). So draw that line down the middle of your journal page, and start thinking. What are the good things about doing this? What are the bad? Go. We'll wait.

Seriously. There's no rush. This stuff takes time.

. . . .Okay. How does it look? Maybe something like this?

PROS

★ I'm here, I'm queer, and now I don't have to hide or fake anything! Yes!

★ Maybe I will inspire others to come out at my school and create a new, beautiful community.

★ My friends will finally know all of me. Whew! Huge sigh of relief.

★ I can go on dates!

★ Smooches!

★ I can meet other queer people and build an affirming and accepting community.

CONS

★ What if I can't find a date?

★ I might be rejected by friends, peers, or teachers.

★ I may get bullied.

★ Someone from school might out me to my parents, siblings, church leaders, etc.

★ What if I don't fit in with the queer crowd at my school?

⭐ What if my school kicks me out or fails to keep me safe?

Deciding which of these factors is most important to you can take some time. Think over this list for a bit. What worries you the most? What are you most excited about? Based on your situation—the kind of school you go to, your principal, your teachers, your friends, and other kids at school—what pros or cons seem particularly likely to happen?

Trust your instincts.

⭐ WHO DO I TELL FIRST?

So, you've weighed your options and . . . *drum roll* . . .

You're coming out at school! Yay!

But how? And who are you going to tell first? How can you be prepared for the inevitable drama and gossip?

If you're not comfortable making a school-wide declaration or unfurling a rainbow flag across your locker and letting everyone jump to their own queer conclusions . . . that's definitely okay. Lots of us don't *start* with telling literally everyone.

There are generally two places to start when coming out at school:

1) **TELLING A TRUSTWORTHY CLASSMATE IS A GREAT FIRST STEP.** Make a list of people in your classes whom you trust, and who are going to respect your privacy. Don't just pick the people you like spending time with. Be discerning, and avoid the gossips as much as possible.

1) **SPEAK WITH A TRUSTED TEACHER, SCHOOL COUNSELOR, OR ADMINISTRATOR.** This might seem terrifying, but many teachers and administrators will happily support and champion their LGBTQ+ students. They can also help you talk

through your concerns about being out at school, especially if you're trans or nonbinary and there are bathroom, locker room, or other policy matters that will need to be addressed. Having an authority figure at your school to keep an eye out for bullying and to advocate on your behalf can be incredibly helpful.

> Please *don't* find an out LGBTQ+ person that you don't actually know and tell them first. You might think you can tru*st them bec*ause they're LGBTQ+, but the fact is that people you already know and trust are much safer. Don't make assumptions about other people—queer or not.

★ SO, WHAT DO I SAY?

We've talked a bit about this before, but we'll say it again. There's no one way to express your identity and orientation. And in fact, you're likely still discovering what labels and language you prefer. That's just fine. You don't have to have everything perfectly figured out before you talk to someone.

It can be helpful to have a couple general labels or words to use as you describe yourself. You might be comfortable and knowledgeable enough already for "I'm transgender and I've always known." Or you might need to start with a more general statement, like "I'm not sure if I'm bi or pan, but I know I'm not straight, and I'm still learning what that means." The best advice we have is: Be as direct and honest as possible. That will give you confidence in your identity, even if you're not set in stone about what your queer identity really is at this or any moment.

You can be honest without being absolutely certain, and doing so will help others understand you in the best way they can.

★ OKAY, BUT . . . MY SCHOOL IS REALLY NOT GOING TO ACCEPT THIS

Depending on where you live and what your school environment is like, coming out may not actually register on the school drama radar. Lots of young people are out. Lots of schools have Gay-Straight Alliance groups (GSAs), queer support groups, or connections to other LGBTQ+ networks. If you're in such a place, good for you. Enjoy it.

But there are still far too many schools that don't accept LGBTQ+ students. This is especially true (tragically) at faith-based or private schools. Only twenty states have laws that explicitly prohibit bullying on the basis of sexual orientation and gender identity, and others ban any education about LGBTQ+ matters. And those laws only cover public schools. Religious and private schools get to make their own sets of standards entirely. Do some research to find out whether your school has any policies about accepting and protecting LGBTQ+ students. Being in a school that does not affirm your whole self is awful, but we know it may be a reality many of you face.

If your school isn't going to accept you or keep you safe, it's okay to simply not come out. That may not feel great, but you don't have to feel ashamed or guilty about not being out at school. If coming out at school jeopardizes your education, your safety, or your mental and emotional health, then don't come out.

When it comes to school, be smart. Be discerning. Set (and keep!) boundaries for your interactions with others. You don't have to tell anyone anything, and remember that you can walk away at any time. High school might feel like everything right now, but graduation is just a few years away!

★ BEWARE THE GOSSIPS!

Teens (okay, people in general) looooove to gossip. When you come out, you've gotta be prepared for the rumor mill to start churning. (Let's be honest: us queer folks have been known to enjoy a bit of gossip too.) No matter what kind of school you attend—public or private, religious or not—there's gonna be people who gossip. So before coming out, you should be at least somewhat prepared for how to tackle the gossips.

When taking on the talkers, have a plan and be strategic. Some options include:

- ★ Engage with the rumor starters or spreaders head-on. ("Yes. I'm queer. Get over it!")

- ★ Completely ignore them (because, screw them!).

- ★ Have a go-to one-liner response to anyone who needs it. (This could be as simple as "Back off!")

- ★ Have supportive friends or teachers prepared to stand up for you.

If you're relying on the support of friends or teachers to deal with gossip, plan ahead with these people. Be specific about what is okay for them to say and what is not. Depending on whether you're out, and how far out, you'll want to have this conversation early with your closest supporters. Because they'll want to be there for you and defend you. Let them know how they can do those things best.

Remember, you are not obligated to answer all or any questions people throw at you. This is your story and you're in charge of how it gets told.

★ WHAT IF SOMEONE STRAIGHT-UP ASKS ME IF I'M QUEER?

Like we said, teenagers love to gossip. Even if you're not already out at school, you might be hearing rumors about your own identity, or someone might even ask you straight to your face.

This can be difficult to navigate. Whether you're ready to come out or not, you certainly don't want to be put on the spot about it unexpectedly. So, what to do when someone asks? Lie to protect yourself? Be honest and face the consequences? Are there any other options?!

Yes. First, set your boundaries. Know what you do and don't want to share about yourself. Remember, you don't owe anyone an answer, even if they directly ask you if you're queer. It's okay to walk away, to ignore them, or to tell them to back off or that it's none of their business. If they continue to press you, verbally or physically, for an answer, this is bullying. Yep, it is. And you can report it. If it's persistent or makes you feel unsafe or targeted, please address the bullying with teachers and administrators. That doesn't mean you have to come out to those teachers or anyone. It means you're keeping yourself—and very likely others—safe.

Whatever circumstances might come up that put you in the spotlight, remember: you do not have to share anything you do not want to share. That means, yes, you can lie to keep yourself safe.

★ A WORD FOR OUR TRANS AND NONBINARY FRIENDS

You're probably going to run into some unique challenges as you decide to come out at school. If you're coming out as trans or nonbinary, this may affect physical elements of your school experience. Whether it's bathrooms, locker rooms, sports teams, or sex ed classes, there are just some practical matters that will likely need to be addressed.

Addressing these issues for some will be easy-peasy, and for others it will . . . not be. Before you come all the way out as trans or nonbinary, it's a really good idea to talk with an administrator at your school, if you feel safe doing so.

You do not have to tell any more people than you're comfortable with, but having institutional support with you on this journey will be important. You are not alone!

That said, before going to an administrator, you might:

- ★ Begin by telling a trusted, safe adult at school.

- ★ Tell a friend or teacher who you know will use your name and pronouns from the get-go.

- ★ If you are out to a parent, ask them to go with you as you talk to school administrators.

This is another good time to remind everyone, but especially trans folks, to do your research. Find out if your school has a Gender Support Plan, and if they don't—and you're comfortable doing so—advocate for one, or ask your friends to do so. (For more on Gender Support Plans, see the "What about Bathrooms?" section of this book). Talking to your school administrators will be a lot easier if you already know your school, local, and state policies.

★ SOMETIMES WAITING IS BEST

If this sounds like a lot of work and attention, and you're the kind of person who'd rather avoid those things (either to focus on your grades or just because you *don't like* work and attention), that's just fine! Lots of queer teens don't come out at school beyond telling their closest friends. If that feels like the best, safest option for you, wonderful. Do that.

High school can feel like a long time when you're in the middle of it. But then suddenly it just . . . ends. In a few years, you'll gain much more control over your life. Until then, be safe and smart, and surround yourself with affirming voices where you can.

★ LAST THOUGHT

School might feel like a minefield after reading this. But so often this isn't the case at all! Many queer teens find their strongest community at school, especially if they can't be out at home or at church. School is where they have freedom to explore their interests and passions, express themselves through dress, participate in or even host rallies and support groups for peers, and advocate for the larger queer community. This may be true for you too! We're not going to pretend that coming out at school isn't scary. But so much life, opportunity, and community may be waiting to welcome you with open arms. Be smart, and if and when you can, be bold. Trust that you're not alone, even at school.

> **Olivia, 21:**
>
> I didn't come out in school. I lived in a rural, conservative town and went to a small Christian school. I was terrified that someone would find out my secret and I would be expelled. I was terrified of what everyone thought of me. And because of that, the person I was at school wasn't the real me.
>
> Once I left school, I moved away from that small-minded town and into the city to go to university. I slowly came to realize that the people around me now were different from before. When I came out in my second year of college, it was so not a big deal that I was shocked. Most of the people I knew were straight and it didn't make any difference to

them. They were supportive and the only thing that changed was how much better I felt. I started going to my university's LGBTQ+ club and got to know other queer people.

I also reconnected with my childhood best friend and turns out she was gay too. We'd gone through the same thing at the same time, thinking we were alone. But we weren't.

If you have come out at school and it went badly, or you can't come out because it's not safe, as much as school feels like your whole life—it's only a very small part of it. And the world is so wide and accepting, and you'll find your place in it in time.

SHOULD I COME OUT AT CHURCH? (DOUBLE GULP!?!)

Here's our stance: Coming out is good. Being able to live authentically and without shame is what we want for you and every queer person in the whole world. *But.*

But we have to admit that there are times when the best advice we can give is three words we wish we never had to say: "Don't come out."

Not coming out can be the smartest, safest decision sometimes, and we would never, ever, ever, ever, EVER, *EVER* encourage someone to come out in a dangerous environment. For many queer Christians (heartbreaking as it is), the most dangerous place to come out is church.

Of course, that's not always the case. For a lot of queer teens, deciding whether or not to come out at church will be no harder than coming out at school.

Some will actually find church *easier.* There are so many affirming and loving churches today, and if you're in one, good for you. You're evidence of a sometimes hard-to-acknowledge truth: we've come a long way. There are dozens of denominations that openly and proudly affirm queer Christians. If you're in such a church, you might not need us for much here. If you're not, read on.

★ WHY IS CHURCH DIFFERENT?

It's true that LGBTQ+ Americans have seen a lot of progress toward acceptance. But that fact doesn't mean anything if *you* don't get to benefit. Until everyone is free to be themselves, everywhere, we still have a long way to go.

If you belong to a faith community that does not accept queer people, or if you're not 100 percent sure, there are some important differences between church and school you should be aware of.

One major difference is that if you go to public school, you have legal rights and protections that do not extend to church. And while some states (though not nearly enough) have specific laws protecting queer people against discrimination, churches don't always have to follow them.

That's why you need to do some research before coming out at church. Find the positions of your denomination, and your church leadership. Both of those things are usually available online. Check out Church Clarity (see the resource list at the back of this book) to see if your church or others like it have clear statements regarding LGBTQ+ affirmation.

Depending on who you have already come out to, you may want to talk to friends or family about whether to come out to your church. A trusted, adult perspective can be useful for thinking out the pros and cons of any big decision regarding your identity.

And remember, there's no wrong answer to the question, "Should I come out?"

★ EVERY CHURCH IS DIFFERENT

You know that thing about people? How God made us all individual and unique? Well, that's true of every church, too. All churches are unique because every congregation is composed of unique individuals. That seems pretty obvious, but it's so important to remember when you're thinking about coming out at church.

After you've researched your church's values and your denomination's teaching, remember that these official positions are not equal to individual beliefs. If you belong to an open and affirming church, it's still likely there are a few bigots in the pews. And if you belong to a church that refuses to affirm people, well, it's still possible that there are allies close by.

> 55% of Evangelical Protestants think queerness should be discouraged. That's awful! But 36% believe it should be accepted, and that is way more than zero.

Don't make assumptions about the people around you. That goes both ways: Don't assume no one will love and affirm you in your church, but don't assume someone will without evidence to back it up.

★ KNOW YOUR TRUTH

Before you come out at church, you should know your truth as best as you are able.

We've already talked about how queer identities can shift over time. You don't need to be 100 percent certain about your queerness, ever. But when it comes to church, it will be helpful to have at least some answer to the *What am I?* question beforehand.

This is especially important if you know, or even think,

> The *What am I?* question doesn't have to be fixed forever at this point. It can and will change, which you can both know and choose not to reveal. You own this process.

your church community rejects queerness. If you were to say, for example, "I think I might be gay," some adults will very likely think, "We need to take action so these thoughts don't take root."

Often, it's a lot easier to say "I think" or "I might be" than it is to say "I am." But hear this, please: In many churches, "I think" will lead to conversion therapy (be it a camp or pray-the-gay-away intervention or a specialized therapist—any attempt to change you is conversion therapy).

It's horrible we have to say this to you, but "I think" easily becomes "I'm not sure," and that can lead to dangerous outcomes.

Reminder:

> *Conversion therapy, in any form, is wrong.*
>
> *It doesn't work.*
>
> *It hurts people.*

Most importantly: *You don't need conversion therapy because nothing is wrong with you. You are queerfully and wonderfully made.*

Any adult (and we mean ANY adult) who tries to change who you are is not an ally and is not acting with your best interests in mind. If you think your church is going to attempt to change your identity, we recommend not coming out at church. You don't owe anyone anything.

★ WEIRD (OR WORSE) CONVERSATIONS

If you do come out at church, we'd like to give you a heads-up: you'll probably end up in some awkward conversations.

Because people are nosy ("How long have you known?"). And people love to gossip ("Did you know that Pastor Sheila's cousin's babysitter's friend Harold is gay?"). And worst of all, when it comes to queer youth, people lack appropriate boundaries ("So who is your crush?").

It doesn't matter if they *think* they're being supportive or not; you have the right to your privacy.

When you are approached, here are a few options for you:

- Walk away. This works every time.

- Say, "I'd rather not talk about this." Many people will be just fine with this.

- Say, "That's not an appropriate question." This is more direct, but it's also educational for the other person involved. (They honestly probably don't realize they're being inappropriate because no one has ever told them! Get it together, cis-hets!)

- Change the subject. "Are you coming to my spoken-word poetry reading this Thursday?" Deflection is better than rejection.

- Walk away. This. Works. Every. Time.

★ LAST THOUGHT

We can't help but repeat this point: Everything in this chapter depends on your personal context and the church you go to. It's hard to give clear guidance on coming out at church, so we're going to wrap up here with a universal message to all queer people: Prioritize your safety.

You can get away from most awkward or uncomfortable situations by simply saying you'd rather not talk about it, because many people are decent, caring, and kind. But *sometimes* they're not. *Sometimes*, an authority figure may put you in a harmful situation. Whatever your situation, prioritize your safety over everything else.

If you ever find yourself in an unsafe, harmful, or inappropriate situation at your church, we're so sorry. Remember: God loves you, you are perfect, and you have the right to do what you need to do to stay safe.

> **Kate, 20:**
>
> Honestly, coming out as nonbinary and queer at church was an extremely anxiety-provoking experience. I was worried about how people would react, and whether they would use the name and pronouns I asked them to use. My church family has always been amazing at showing me unconditional love and support, and this instance was no different. I felt a huge sense of relief, like I was finally able to be my full self around those I loved and worshipped with.
>
> I think it is important to remember that it is your choice whether you come out at church or not, and if you do, when and how. You don't owe anything to anyone. Each person's coming out is different. When you're coming out to more than a few people, there's no "normal" way to do it. Find a way that makes you most comfortable. Take your time. The people who will love you will be there whenever you are ready.
>
> There will likely be someone who doesn't understand, or who has questions about your identity. If you can, be patient and answer them. It might be hard, but stand up for yourself. You deserve to be respected. Most importantly, you are loved unconditionally by the God who designed and created you, and who knows you better than anyone.

DO I HAVE TO ANSWER EVERYONE'S QUESTIONS?

Being out means you'll get questions.

Some questions will be friendly, respectful, and genuinely curious—but others could be awkward, or worse. Regardless of why someone asks you about you, you have zero obligation to answer any questions from anyone. Your life, including every aspect of your queerness, is your business and no one else's.

That does not mean that you should put up a wall between you and your family or friends or church community. In some cases, you might *want* to talk. Talking helps. It helps get us out of our heads and helps us feel understood by those closest to us. It all depends on who's asking, what they're asking, and how you want to respond (if you want to at all).

Here are some things you might think about as different groups of people come at you with their questions.

★ PARENTS

We've already talked a lot about your parents. But just a reminder: You are not responsible for educating your parents. They should do their own work, be it with a pastor, therapist, or PFLAG group. (Formerly known as Parents and Friends of Lesbians and Gays, PFLAG is the largest national LGBTQ+ support group for families and friends of queer people.) But you know parents. Right? They could probably use a hand. And there's a lot riding on what your parents learn in these early stages of your coming-out process. If we leave them to their own internet research, who knows what they'll find?

- ★ Help them in ways that are safe and appropriate. Many parents will want to talk about and learn to understand their child. But if conversations veer into topics like conversion therapy or threats about living in "their house," they should be talking to someone else.

- ★ Point them to quality resources and affirming materials, such as PFLAG, Queer Grace, and Reconciling Works. There are many more listed in the back of this book.

★ TEACHERS, SCHOOL ADMINISTRATORS

There are very, *very* few questions that are appropriate for a teacher or administrator to ask a student about their queer identity. In some school districts, any discussion of the subject at all is banned. You should be leading any discussion with your school, and not the other way around.

If you have a teacher you trust, and who offers a safe and helpful voice in school, okay.

If you have a teacher who is asking a lot of specific, unusual questions, or taking too much interest in your life, stay away from them and tell your parents or counselor.

★ ADULTS AT CHURCH

Like school, there aren't many questions about your queer identity that should be coming from the adults in your church, whether or not your church welcomes and affirms queer people. But if your church does *not* subscribe to queer-affirming theology, answering questions can be extra dangerous.

Feel free to walk away (this works every time) or just say something like, "I don't really want to talk about that right now."

Be safe.

★ FRIENDS, SCHOOL BUDS

All we can recommend here is that you use your best judgment. As you get further out of the closet, people are going to find out and have questions. Answer the questions you're comfortable answering, from people you're comfortable giving information to. One way you can decide whether or not to engage with the question is to take a look at what's motivating it. Does the question seem to be coming from a genuine interest in knowing you better, or is it a gossipy, invasive question from someone looking for juicy details?

★ RED FLAGS

Here's a word we wish you didn't need to know: *grooming*. We're not talking about brushing your teeth or shaving your legs here, dears. We are talking about bad, *bad*, *BAD* people.

grooming: verb
> the process in which an adult develops a
> friendship with a child, particularly through
> the internet, with the intention of having a
> sexual relationship.

There are adults out there who are looking for vulnerable young people to take advantage of. It's not uncommon for these adults to target queer youth who feel isolated from their families. And it's also not uncommon for these adults to be in churches and schools. Pastors, priests, youth leaders. Counselors, teachers, bus drivers. This kind of behavior is rare, but it can come from anywhere.

And it is terrible. No matter what, every time.

But it happens, and it's important that you know about these risks when interacting with adults. Grooming will often start with seemingly innocent questions from a seemingly concerned adult who takes a special interest in a young person looking for support. Often, after building trust in face-to-face interactions, they will look to communicate over text or online, where they will increase the amount of communication and get more personal in their interactions. If these predators work at their target's school or church, they will try to create scenarios where they can be alone with the young person.

You might think we're being overly cautious, or that this can't happen at your church or school, or even in your family, but the truth is many targets of grooming don't realize it's happening until too late. If there is an adult in your life who . . .

* makes you nervous to be around,

* asks weird or sketchy questions,

* asks for personal contact info,

* shows up in your social media feed,

* requests photos of any kind,

* finds reasons to get you alone, . . .

you need to protect yourself.

Don't answer questions you're not comfortable answering. Never be alone with them. Never send them (or *any* adult, really) photos. *And most importantly, tell another adult.* An affirming, trustworthy adult needs to know, whether it's a parent, a teacher, a counselor, a youth pastor, or any other adult you trust and feel safe around. What is happening is not your fault; you have done nothing wrong (even if the predator says you have or that you'll get in trouble). Tell an adult. Please.

If you suspect you are being targeted by an adult, it's crucial that you don't try to handle it alone. Listen to your gut; follow your instincts. God loves you. We love you. Be safe.

★ LAST THOUGHT

Anything you share could get shared again outside of your presence. Unless you are talking to a reliable secret-keeper, expect things to spread.

MY CHURCH IS NOT GOING TO LIKE IT IF I COME OUT. WHAT THEN?

Predicting what will happen after you come out is very, very hard to do (only God knows for sure, right?). Though many churches (and individuals within those churches) are becoming more queer-affirming, it's also the case that those churches that are not affirming are becoming *even more* aggressive and outspoken against LGBTQ+ people.

Which means many of you are facing this scary question. Whether you know for certain or suspect that your church is non-affirming, in the end it doesn't really matter when it comes to being queer at church.

Whatever circumstances led you to a position of uncertainty, fear, guilt, shame, doubt, or any other feelings you might have, let us be the first to say, *we are so sorry*. If you feel these things, then your community, your church itself, has let you down. But know that God hasn't. God sees, loves, and cherishes you for exactly who you are. God loves you *because of* your queerness, not in spite of it, no matter what your pastors or teachers are telling you.

So, if you have not come out at church, and you recognize the risks of doing so are real, this may seem obvious, but:

Please do not come out.

We don't like to recommend people stay closeted. After accepting one's LGBTQ+ identity, it's natural to want to share it. Meaning, the decision *not* to come out is often just as emotionally difficult as the decision *to* come out. It's normal to want to be out and proud of who you are—we get that. You may also find yourself wanting to change your church's stance on LGBTQ+ affirmation by coming out. You may want to spark conversations and encourage others to grow past their stereotypes. And it's certainly possible that coming out at your church could result in some desperately overdue change. So if you're safe, secure, and supported by your family, go ahead and stir the waters!

BUT . . .

★ WE HAVE TO BE REAL

Most churches that are anti-queer are unlikely to change. That's a simple fact. They are far more likely to put their efforts into changing *you*. So before you decide to come out, or take up an activist role at your church, realistically ask yourself a couple things:

- ★ What risks to my health and safety should I expect at church or home?

- ★ Will I be expected to undergo conversion therapy or other "treatments" if I come out?

- ★ Will this church give me a real chance to bring change, or will my voice (or worse, will *I*) be quickly pushed out?

Your desire to see change in church is important (*so* important) and admirable (*so, so* admirable). But you have to keep your safety in mind.

> A huge majority of LGBTQ+ young people are not out at church. According to the Human Rights Campaign, only 8% of queer youth have come out in their church community. A lot of you just are not going to come out at church, and that's OKAY! It doesn't say anything about you, your queerness, your courage, or your faithfulness.

★ IT'S NOT YOUR RESPONSIBILITY

Christians have a lot of sayings, some of which aren't helpful (or even true). One of these phrases is, "God put me here for a reason." Ahem, we see you, Queen Esther. And while we would love for you to march into the throne room with your queenly crown and majestic cape and boldly stand up for your people, well . . .

That may not happen. And that's *okay*. The truth is, God does not "put" us in harm's way to teach us something (or to teach others through us). If you are feeling pressured for any reason—whether that pressure comes from others or from yourself—because you've been told queerness is contrary to God's will, *it's not*. You are God's precious, loved child.

God didn't make you queer *so that* you could be coerced, hurt, or dehumanized, just to prove a point. It's not *your* responsibility to change someone's heart. God does that.

God also gives us wisdom and discernment. That means that you should trust yourself when things feel wrong. So, weigh your options wisely and make a safe decision. It's not easy to withstand pressure from our faith community, but strengthen yourself with supportive and affirming friends, family, and resources.

★ BUT I REALLY, REALLY WANT TO COME OUT HERE

If you're just dead set on coming out at your church, take some wise steps. Find an advocate in your church who can help you field questions and stand up on your behalf. Ask them if they think it's wise for you to come out to the pastor(s) and leadership, or if you should wait or not come out at all. While getting the advice of others can be helpful, remember, *it's your choice*. You're not being dishonest, deceptive, or weak by not coming out. You're actually taking ownership of your journey and who goes on it with you.

★ LAST THOUGHT

We wish we could tell you for sure whether to come out at your church. But we can't because we don't know your church. But *you do*. Trust yourself; trust that feeling in the pit of your stomach. You *know* what to do.

> **Omar, 24:**
>
> I think deciding to come out at church all depends on your church family, and even then, it's a very difficult question. Growing up, I came out to many people at my church. Sometimes it went well, other times it didn't. And the hard part is, there's not always a good way of knowing whether or not coming out to someone will end positively. Because, at the end of the day, their reaction is beyond our control. In the moment, every time I came out to someone it seemed to be the "right" decision. And I still stand by that, even if their reaction was painful. Because making a decision like that has to feel "right" for you. I know at times it feels like a minefield out there; you don't always know who will hurt you. But closing yourself off is never the answer to that potential pain.

YOU DON'T HAVE TO COME OUT

We've said this a few times, but it's worth repeating. One. Last. Time. YOU DO NOT HAVE TO COME OUT.

Wait until you're out of the house. Wait until you're out of college. Wait as long as you want. It's not up to anyone but you, so if you want to wait, we hope you do.

You can't make a wrong decision on when you come out. You are beloved, queerfully and wonderfully made, no matter who knows what.

Shayla, 28:

I came out in my mid-twenties and it's been a lot of emotional whiplash for me. Relationships that I thought were set in stone and unconditional have changed a lot. Others have strengthened. It's a weird process, but everything will be okay.

In my teens, a bad reaction would have affected my life much more since I still relied on my family so much. But when I did come out, I lived a few states away and had my own apartment and my own life. So while rejection hurt a lot, it wasn't a catastrophe.

This is just to say that if you feel like you aren't ready to come out, don't worry. I wasn't, and there were plenty of pros to coming out later. If you feel like you need to come out sooner rather than later, and you're safe to do so, there are plenty of pros to that, too. I never believed people who told me "Do things in your own time," but they were right. It's also been hard to believe people who say, "Things get better," but the longer I'm out, the more I realize that it's true.

INTERLUDE:

Queer Icons of Christianity (A Short List)

PERPETUA AND FELICITY (DIED AROUND 203)

This story comes straight from the diaries of Saint Perpetua herself. Perpetua and Felicity were North African women of unequal status. Perpetua was a married noblewoman, Felicity a slave. Their stories cross in a prison in Carthage (in Tunisia, today), where they were awaiting their execution as part of a public military celebration on the birthday of Emperor Septimus Severus.

Were Perpetua and Felicity romantically involved? Of course, we don't know. What we can say is this: there was an emotional connection that ran very deep in the women, they exchanged a kiss as they were being murdered, and they died in each other's arms.

Today, many Christians consider the women to be the patron saints of same-sex couples.

SAINT SEBASTIAN (DIED 288)

Saint Sebastian is also a sainted queer icon, killed by the Roman empire—though we have no direct evidence of him being queer, per se. Sebastian was a soldier in the Roman army, killed on the orders of Emperor Diocletian after Sebastian converted to Christianity. That's about what we know of Saint Sebastian. So, what gives with the gay icon thing?

To answer that we have to jump ahead 1,500 years, to when the Italian Baroque painter Guido Reni created seven paintings of Saint Sebastian. Paintings that are . . . well, they're pretty hot. They portray a young man, baby-faced and rosy-cheeked, bound at the wrists, in a skimpy loin cloth, punctured by arrows. And his face? Well, it's ecstatic.

By the nineteenth century, Sebastian was the central figure in gay religious cults. Oscar Wilde (another gay icon) adopted Sebastian's name while in exile, and today, the LGBTQ+ community puts him on everything from magazine covers to rainbow pride merchandise.

HILDEGARD OF BINGEN (DIED 1179)

Mystic. Theologian. Poet. Painter. Artist. Scientist. Lesbian?

Okay, we can't be sure about that last one, and using modern terminology on classical people is a bit unfair. But Hildegard was a strong advocate for women, and she advanced interests in women's health and sexuality. She founded many monasteries and convents, and her work makes clear that she had strong emotional relationships with other women.

One of those women was named Richardis. She lived in the same monastery as Hildegard, and their connection—whatever it looked like—is indisputable. The emotional attachment between the two women is the stuff of legend for queer people today.

Tragically, Richardis died at twenty-eight years old, and her death is said to have inspired Hildegard's work until her own death, twenty-eight years later.

JOAN OF ARC (DIED 1431)

Among the most famous of martyrs and medieval saints, Joan of Arc was—we can't stress this enough—*so* queer. At least she seems that way today. Joan was prone to sharing beds with other girls and cross-dressing, and her fellow soldiers referred to her as a "monstrous woman."

Still a teenager at the time of her death, Joan was an uneducated, illiterate peasant. When she was thirteen, she started having visions of saints who brought her messages from God, telling her she would lead the French to defeat the English in battle. At sixteen, she made the case for herself as God's chosen victor for France, reportedly telling military

leaders, "I must be at the king's side. There is no help if not from me." Imagine a poor girl in boy's clothes saying this to today's leaders. Whoa. Anyway, she convinced the men of her kingdom and led the French to incredible victories, resulting in a truce between the nations, before her eventual capture.

All of this, it turns out, was a big no-no for teenage girls in the 1400s. For her efforts, she was burned at the stake. Today, Joan of Arc is a saint in the church, and she is an icon of LGBTQ+ ferocity. A warrior-saint woman in full male armor, taking names. Yes pleeeezz.

MICHELANGELO (DIED 1564)

Most famously, Michelangelo is the Renaissance painter who spent four years painting the ceiling of the Sistine Chapel in Rome. Less famously, Michelangelo was super gay, and he wrote lots of super-gay poetry. His poetry is so obviously gay, in fact, that when it was published in 1623 by Michelangelo's grand-nephew, the pronouns were changed to make the poems hetero-normie and straight. They were not corrected until 1893.

Talk about erasure.

The randiest poems Michelangelo wrote were to a young nobleman named Tommaso dei Cavalieri, so feel free to Google those. Unlike the rest of this list, it's basically impossible to deny that Michelangelo was queer, and nobody (well, almost nobody) really bothers trying.

IS MY CHURCH'S TEACHING ABUSIVE? AND CAN I LEAVE IT?

All right, we've been talking about church for a while here, and we're getting close to almost getting to the end of our chapters about being a Church Queer. But hang with us because we still have some very real stuff to talk about. For queer Christians, it is pretty much one of the, if not *the*, trickiest part of life to navigate. So take a breather, maybe do some stretches, and let's get back to the tough stuff.

Okay. You ready? Let's go there.

★ IT'S TIME WE TALKED ABOUT RELIGIOUS ABUSE

This is a tough one, but it's important. Religious abuse is all too common, and it comes in many forms. In conservative, non-affirming churches, abusive teaching and behavior can be very obvious. But a lot of churches, including progressive or mainline churches, can be harmful too. They're just better at hiding it. As you navigate the church waters as a queer Christian, chances are you're going to run into religious abuse. If you haven't already.

In case you don't know what we're talking about, let's define religious abuse. Religious abuse can look and sound like a lot of different things:

* **Any teaching that uses "God," "Scripture," etc. to shame, belittle, or isolate LGBTQ+ people.** This could be a sermon on sexual purity or an off-handed joke about Adam and Steve. It doesn't matter how it happens—it's abuse.

* **Threats of damnation:** "You're going to HELL because you're GAY!" (First of all, you're not. Second of all, no one judges but the Lord.)

* **Oversexualizing LGBTQ+ people:** "If you're queer, all you think about is *sex*." (Okay, again first of all, not true, and second of all . . . thinking about sex is fun and not a problem!)

* **Public rebuke:** Preaching to a congregation that gays are evil, wrong, unnatural, while *knowing* that a queer person is in the pews. Or even face-to-face confrontations.

- ★ **Outing someone:** In any circumstance, but especially in front of a church. This sometimes happens in prayers for the congregation. And no pastor should ever out anyone. It is the picture of abusive behavior.

- ★ **Erasure:** "I can't imagine being attracted to men *and* women. So that's not real." (Well, we can't imagine being a closed-minded prig, so guess you're not real, either.)

- ✹ **Attributing every part of your "failure" or "sins" to your queer identity:** "You're depressed/anxious/guilty . . ." or "You drink/party/smoke because you're queer." (Note the quotation marks around failure and sins because those are NOT failures or sins.)

The above list contains a lot of obvious examples of religious abuse. You will know—and feel—when these things happen in your church. But also know that religious abuse doesn't have to come from the pulpit. Anti-queer sentiments are in fact often cloaked from church preaching, from a church's literature or website, and from their youth programs. It may be more subtle, and may come from volunteers or staff, and *not* the pastoral team.

Religious abuse can take subtler forms:

- ★ Never mentioning queer identities, in any context, including sacraments.

- ★ Using policy statements to enforce anti-LGBTQ+ theology—like not conducting or renting space for same-sex weddings

- ★ Constantly conducting gender-specific activities, small groups, etc. "Boys to the left, girls to the right!"

* Not using appropriate language, names, pronouns, etc. Purposefully deadnaming and misgendering are always abuse.

* Enforcing and teaching gender essentialism (the idea that there is one right way to be a man or a woman). The concepts behind gender essentialism, like the idea that boys-will-be-boys or the Proverbs 31 woman, have been shown to be wrong everywhere, in every time.

> Gender essentialism is not just a transgender problem. The root of homophobia is often gender-based too. Gay men are too feminine. Lesbians are too masculine. Bi folks are too . . . both? That doesn't make sense, and it shouldn't anyway because this is all garbage. If gender essentialism is correct, LGBTQ+ people are just "wrong" when it comes to being a person. Even the Bible does not depict one way to be masculine and one way to be feminine.

★ WHAT SHOULD I DO ABOUT RELIGIOUS ABUSE?

First of all, we want you to call religious abuse what it is: WRONG. God does not want you to be treated this way. Church should be welcoming, accepting, and loving. If it isn't, they are the problem, not you.

You got that? Good, we'll say it again anyway. Religious abuse is wrong. But it is pervasive. It's deeply rooted, and it creates institutions that are oh-so-difficult to change. If you've grown up hearing abusive teaching your entire life, you're likely carrying around incredible guilt and shame, the weight of which can really, really way you down. It can become a burden on a queer person, even making you think you deserve it.

Dear friend, what they are saying is not true. You don't deserve to be the target of abusive theology or behavior at church. Religious abuse is the opposite of Jesus' message. It's time to recognize and let go of those lies. Start believing the truth God says about you: You ARE loved, you ARE who you were created to be, you ARE enough.

Okay, now that we've established what religious abuse looks like, it's time to figure out what to do about it. Like everything in church, your context is crucial. But here are a few options to consider if you are in a church that openly or tacitly rejects LGBTQ+ people:

- ★ First: Recognize the kind and level of religious abuse you are experiencing. Knowing what it looks like in your context will help you understand what you need to do in response.

- ★ If your parents support and affirm your queerness, talk to them about how you are feeling. They may recommend something that surprises you—maybe a different church or, if it's a specific person or group at your church causing a problem, they might be willing to talk to them about the problem on your behalf.

- ★ Be aware of what forms conversion therapy can take. If what you're experiencing at church is a form of this "therapy," and the practice is banned in your state, you can (and absolutely should!) report it. If conversion therapy is legal in your state, you might have to fight against it on your own behalf. Arm yourself with the data on conversion therapy (it's in this book! See _____) and tell your parents just how dangerous the practice is.

★ LEAVE! Yes, it's okay to leave your church. Maybe doing so is painful, or maybe it's a relief. Either way, your safety is more important than not offending others.

★ If you want to, find an affirming congregation that will welcome and accept you. We're not going to pretend it's easy joining a new church, especially if you're still healing from the abuse of another one. If you need to take a break from church altogether for a bit, that's okay. But know that there are many wonderful, beautiful, godly congregations waiting to welcome, celebrate, and love you with open arms.

Rox, 24:

For every person who rejected me, there are ten people who supported me. My family rejected me, so I found a new family. My friends rejected me, so I found new friends. My church rejected me, so I found a new church. The important thing is: Never stop searching for the people, family, friends, and community who will be there for you, love you, and support you, no matter what. They're out there; just keep looking.

WHAT IF MY CONGREGATION IS FULL OF ANTI-LGBTQ+ BIGOTS?

Well first off, that sounds like a terrible church and we're so sorry you're in it! *Bigot* can sound like a harsh word, but it actually refers to anyone who discriminates against someone based solely on external or unchangeable factors (race, gender, ethnicity, sexual orientation, etc.). We're sure you've run into a few bigots in your time . . .

When it comes to bigotry, one loud, non-affirming voice can make an entire church feel like a dangerous environment. Or maybe it doesn't *feel* dangerous. Maybe bigotry seems like the voice of concerned adults. But these voices around you are harmful. It's okay, even necessary, to admit this.

So now what? How do you fight the power and take down the bigotry?

★ TWO (VERY DIFFERENT) RESPONSES TO BIGOTRY

Bigotry (and discrimination and harassment and intolerance) is as old as human culture. Even Jesus faced intolerance and bigotry for his teaching. Some of this bigotry came from self-righteous Pharisees. In fact, Jesus had some interesting, and quite different, responses when it came to the bigots of his day. Here are some of the tactics he used:

1: LET THEM HAVE IT

On the off chance you have a Bible lying around, take a quick look at Matthew 23. (No, really, go ahead!) You don't have to read very long to see . . . wow, Jesus is *angry*.

Why is Jesus so angry? Well, the religious leaders of his time (the Pharisees) were pretty much the worst. They were allowing injustice and abuse of the common people, all while constantly bragging about how fantastic they were at following God (spoiler: they weren't).

Jesus had had enough. Take a look at some of his insults (and maybe add a few to your repertoire):

* "Child of hell"

* "You blind fools!"

* "You snakes, you brood of vipers!"

* "How can you escape being sentenced to hell?"

* "You are like whitewashed tombs, which on the outside look beautiful, but inside they are full of the bones of the dead and of all kinds of filth."

Yikes.

Jesus, confronted with the bigoted religious know-it-alls of his day, wasn't so meek and mild. Jesus shocked the regular folks of his time by fighting the bigotry of the Pharisees. Jesus upended the religious institution of his day by preaching a message of love, grace, and forgiveness that totally went against the Pharisees' pride and hate. And to do that, sometimes Jesus shouted at bigots.

Sometimes bigotry, injustice, and religious abuse must be

called out. And yes, sometimes fighting bigotry with words and confrontation is the right thing to do. And if it is done wisely, it can be powerful, inspiring, life-changing. Raising our voices draws a crowd, challenges old thinking, and brings down systems of oppression. And, honestly, it feels good.

This approach isn't for everyone, and raising our voices *can* be dangerous. Which means that sometimes, you might prefer to. . .

2: TAKE THE GENTLE APPROACH (LIKE JESUS ALSO DID, AND MORE OFTEN)

Sure, Jesus's insult fest is pretty badass. But if we're going to talk about Jesus, we've got to talk about his *whole* message. Here are a few insights from Jesus that you might have heard about:

✦ "You have heard that it was said, 'An eye for an eye and a tooth for a tooth.' But I say to you, do not resist an evildoer. But if anyone strikes you on the right cheek, turn the other also; and if anyone wants to sue you and take your coat, give your cloak as well." (Matthew 5:38-40)

★ "You have heard that it was said, 'You shall love your neighbor and hate your enemy.' But I say to you, love your enemies and pray for those who persecute you." (Matthew 5:43-44)

✤ "Blessed are you when people revile you and persecute you and utter all kinds of evil against you falsely on my account. Rejoice and be glad, for your reward is great in heaven, for in the same way they persecuted the prophets who were before you." (Matthew 5:11-12)

It might seem like this method is less likely to produce change. But here's the thing: Jesus was wise. He knew that harboring bitterness and anger in our hearts (even if we're angry for a good cause) is only going to cause us pain. Extending forgiveness and love, even when we're not receiving it from others, sets us apart. More importantly, it sets *you* apart. You are modeling for your church, your pastor, the prejudiced loudmouth, and everyone else that love and grace are actually what *they* are called to.

It may be less satisfying in the moment, but it's a powerful act of advocacy on behalf of queer folks everywhere.

There's nothing weak about this kind of love. Think about Martin Luther King Jr., Mother Teresa, Nelson Mandela. Some of the most powerful revolutionaries, visionaries, and change-bringers of our time preached this same message of nonviolence and peace. And they changed history. So, before you start flipping tables in the sanctuary (something Jesus also did!), remember that love and grace are usually much better weapons against hate.

★ PEARLS BEFORE PIGS

There's this weird verse in Matthew where Jesus tells people not to cast their pearls before pigs (or swine, as it were):

"Do not give what is holy to dogs; and do not throw your pearls before swine, or they will trample them under foot and turn and maul you" (Matthew 7:6 NRSV).

Pretty weird, right? Why would you throw your pearls at pigs in the first place?!?

Well, you wouldn't. But what Jesus means here is . . . some folks are not going to change, regardless of what approach you or anyone else takes to their bigotry. You may have received love, grace, and acceptance from God. You may be eager to share this message with others.

But try as we might, we can't *force* anyone to change. No matter how loudly, softly, eloquently, or boldly we speak, some will not have a heart to listen. It might be your mom and dad, a close friend, a pastor, or a random bigot in the pews of your congregation. But these people, these bigots, are out there.

And when you encounter this person, when you realize you're throwing pearls before swine, that is when you walk away. Not in defeat or with your head down. You walk away with grace, forgiveness, and the hope that you have planted a seed in their hearts that will grow long after you are gone.

★ LAST THOUGHT

When you encounter bigotry, discrimination, or hatred, you can stay and argue—or you can protect yourself and walk away. It's okay. Stay confident, knowing that your queerness does not depend on the approval (or disapproval) of others.

WHAT IF MY CONGREGATION IS TOO AFFIRMING? (THIS HAPPENS!)

You may read this question and burst out laughing. *Too* affirming?! As if! I wish! But it happens, and it can be a bit disappointing in its own ways.

Being queer often comes with a sense of individuality and outsider-status that many queer young people (and adults) relish. A church or family that is "too affirming" can make one feel like their queerness is not their own. If you come out, and your parents are proud, your friends are proud, your school is proud, *and* your church is proud, then it might feel like, well, it's too easy! There's nowhere to push the boundaries, to craft

your own self in the fires of straight-cisgender society, or even to make someone a little (just a little) angry.

And, look, we feel a little bad for you. Expressing your queerness should feel good, and being a teen who gets praised at every turn can be, well, a bit annoying. But mostly, we are just so very thankful you're surrounded by so many loving people! Go share that love with some of your queer friends who aren't as lucky as you. You'll have plenty of opportunities to rebel against the system in your future.

WHAT IF MY PASTOR, PARENTS, OR ANYONE TRIES TO MAKE ME STRAIGHT?

If you've come out, you may have experienced others trying to "make you straight." Maybe it is repeated not-so-subtle comments about sin or about what's "natural." Maybe it's a pray-the-gay-away session. Maybe it's appointments with a "therapist" recommended by a pastor or your parents.

All of these abusive interventions are versions of conversion therapy, and no matter what form it takes, conversion therapy is always wrong. The idea that someone could be "made straight" is unfounded, hurtful, and downright dangerous. Yet conversion therapy is a reality for thousands of queer teens. We want you to know how you can respond if you encounter anyone trying to make you straight.

★ WHAT DOES CONVERSION THERAPY LOOK LIKE?

Conversion therapy, also known as "reparative therapy," is any practice aimed at intentionally changing your sexual orientation or gender identity. The practice as we understand it today has been around for a long time (like, since the 1890s, long time) and it's used some pretty shocking (literally) methods.

Back in the (not-so-old) days, homosexuality was considered mental illness and was illegal in a whole lot of countries, including the United States. Many doctors, religious leaders, therapists, and even law enforcement officers recommended conversion therapy to "change" someone from gay to straight. A very common way of "curing" queerness was aversion therapy: Whenever a patient exhibited a same-gender attraction or erotic thought, a facilitator would induce physical nausea and vomiting, or would use an electric shock to "punish" the patient for queer thoughts.

Are you outraged?! We are! Don't worry, this type of therapy has been widely condemned among mental health professionals (because it didn't work—obviously). Conversion therapy looks different nowadays, but the risks are still all too scary. Instead of vomiting and electric shock, today's conversion therapy often uses hypnosis, cognitive or behavioral therapies, sex therapies, medication, or a simple equation of shame + guilt + more shame + threats of damnation.

Conversion therapy is a horrible chapter of queer history, and while the methods have changed, the practice continues. And so does the fight to end it.

★ HOW POPULAR IS CONVERSION THERAPY NOW?

Unfortunately, it's still too common.

* In the US, nearly 700,000 LGBTQ+ adults have undergone conversion therapy at some point in their lives.

* About 350,000 of these received conversion therapy as teenagers.

* An estimated 57,000 youth (ages 13–17) across the US will receive conversion therapy *from religious or spiritual leaders* before they are 18.

Many mental health professionals think the number of teens undergoing conversion therapy is actually much higher than reported, because many are ashamed to admit it or didn't realize their experience qualified as conversion therapy. When the question was re-asked as "Have you ever experienced someone forcing you to change your identity or orientation?" the numbers increased significantly.

★ DOES CONVERSION THERAPY WORK?

Absolutely not.

There has been no credible research (never, not ever) showing that conversion therapy has successfully "changed" someone's sexual orientation. The American Psychological Association (APA) has officially condemned the practice of conversion therapy.

Instead, the APA finds a series of very dangerous outcomes from the practice: family rejection, depression, anxiety, and suicide. Undergoing conversion therapy can cause serious damage to one's mental health and well-being. Some of the scariest numbers out there for LGBTQ+ teens are those linked to undergoing conversion therapy. But we promised not to sugarcoat the facts, and we're sticking to that. Awareness is preparedness!

* Conversion therapy is associated with higher rates of depression, anxiety, family rejection, and suicide.

* LGBTQ+ youth who have undergone conversion therapy are over twice as likely to attempt suicide.

* 57% of transgender and nonbinary youth who have undergone conversion therapy have attempted suicide.

If you're experiencing suicidal thoughts or are thinking of hurting yourself, there is help.

★ **National Suicide Prevention Hotline: 1-800-273-8255**

★ **Crisis Text Line: Text "HOME" to 741741**

★ **Trevor Project LGBTQ+ Support Line: 1-866-488-7386**

★ **Trans Lifeline: 1-877-565-8860**

Conversion therapy . . . *definitely* a very bad thing.

★ WHAT IF MY PARENTS OR PASTOR FORCE ME INTO CONVERSION THERAPY?

First, you need to know the laws around conversion therapy in your state. Bans on conversion therapy are passing in cities and states throughout the United States, and if you're in one of those states, you'll want to know that you are. It's the first line of protection. If you're in a state that outlaws the practice and someone encourages or forces you into it, you absolutely should report it.

Honestly, conversion therapy is so horrible, and the results of it are so dangerous, that if you know it's happening (either to you or to someone else) and you feel comfortable doing so, you should report it. No matter what the laws of your town, city, or state say.

How you report the practice is up to you and what level of comfort you have. You could do something as simple as sending an email to the American Civil Liberties Union, asking them to look into it but not to contact you again. Or you could contact an LGBTQ+ advocacy organization and ask them to create a loud media hubbub over the practice taking place. (If you ask the queer community to show up for you, we'll show up for you. We are HERE FOR YOU!)

Wherever there is conversion therapy, there are queer folks ready to fight it.

★ OKAY . . . BUT WHAT IF I CAN'T ESCAPE CONVERSION THERAPY?

Despite the best efforts of everyone involved in the LGBTQ+ rights movement, some teens will find themselves forced to attend a church, small group, camp, etc. that is actively trying to change their sexual orientation or gender identity.

If you find yourself in this situation, and if it's at all possible, you should *leave that space*. If you are being subjected to conversion therapy at church, you should leave that church. Hopefully your family comes with you, but your safety and security are the top priority. If it's a counselor, a teacher, or a youth leader doing this to you, ask for help finding a new one. There are many queer-affirming therapists and pastors out there, and they can be *wonderful* resources for you.

If refusal to participate in conversion therapy leads to an ultimatum from your parents ("You can't live under this roof unless . . ."), we're very sorry. You're facing some very hard choices. But sometimes you have to make them. Weigh the risks of staying versus leaving. Ask yourself: "Do I have a friend or family member who will let me stay with them?"

There are resources for youth facing homelessness (in the back of this book, and through your state and local LGBTQ+ communities).

And to those of you for whom leaving is not an option, all we can say is . . . just wait it out. This isn't very satisfying, and we're sorry we can't offer you more. But please just hang in there. You'll be eighteen soon. Then, if you want to leave, you can. Until then, surround yourself with affirming voices that counter the messages you're hearing at church or home. See if there are affirming leaders, writers, etc. in your denomination or congregation. These can be amazing supports for you.

Emma, 21:

Not only does my country have laws against queer people and queer relationships, but most of the churches in my hometown also think that being LGBTQ is a mental health issue. It takes a while to heal from thinking for many years that there is something wrong with how you love. I still experience this today from other pastors and leaders in my life. Sometimes, it helps to break out of the environment you're used to in order to have a breakthrough. It happened for me when I decided to reach out to organizations, friends, and families that open doors to the LGBTQ+ community.

Reaching out to those who want to make an effort to understand you better and support you for that can make a huge difference in your life. You don't need any saving. You don't need to "get better."

WHAT IF I WANT TO CHANGE?

Dear one, we would ask you gently, *Why* do you want to change? Is this desire motivated by guilt, shame, embarrassment, or any other voice making you feel not enough? Do you want to change because you believe it will make your family, your parents, maybe even yourself, happier? Do you wish you were "normal" and had an "easy" straight life?

If you're thinking anything like this, we need you to know . . . the voice in your head telling you to change is not God's voice. God says that you are loved, valuable, and *wonderful* just as you are. Your queerness is God's creation, and it is perfect.

Sometimes the hardest challenge isn't receiving acceptance from God or other people; it's receiving acceptance from ourselves. If you find yourself struggling to accept yourself for who you are, we hope that you are able to find a way to let go of that shame. Acceptance is part of your journey, and it might take a while. But don't give up!

Honestly, no matter how much you want to change . . . most likely you're not going to. Learn to love yourself and celebrate yourself as you are now. Loving yourself is a way to affirm God's creation. Believe the truth about yourself: *You are loved. You are valuable. You are enough.* Write this on your bathroom mirror, a sticky note in your car, a tattoo on your forearm! Do what it takes to get this truth inside your mind, heart, and soul. You can't and don't need to change.

WHAT IF I'M ALL ALONE IN A WORLD OF STRAIGHT PEOPLE?

Statistically speaking, you're definitely going to be surrounded by straight, cisgender people (we are a minority, after all).

But good news! Each passing generation has a higher percentage of out queer folks than the one that came before! In fact, one recent study found that only 66 percent of Gen Z youth identified as completely heterosexual. This means a third of your peers might be queer as well.

Nonetheless, sometimes it can seem like you're the only queer person in the whole world (especially if you're not out yet). And though you may be in a particularly straight community, you are not totally alone! You might just have to work a little harder to find your community. Here are a few ways to get started:

* See if your school has a GSA (Gay-Straight Alliance) or other queer support organization. If it does and you're comfortable joining, join! And if it doesn't have one, consider starting one. Become the queer role model you were looking for! (I think Gandhi said that?)

★ See if there's a local LGBTQ+ center, advocacy organization, or other community-based queer group in your area. They often have social events, support groups, and volunteer opportunities that provide healthy, affirming, and fun ways to expand your queer social network.

★ Join an online forum (a *healthy* one, please). Check out queergrace.com, Queer Christian Fellowship, TrevorSpace, or a queer-friendly Tumblr page (there are TONS!).

★ Keep an eye out for events and LGBTQ+ social meetups at your local bookstores, coffee shops, and social media spaces.

★ STRAIGHT PEOPLE AREN'T SCARY (NOT ALL OF THEM, AT LEAST!)

Lots of young queer people feel isolated from the queer community. But remember that your allies are your community, too. We need allies. Your straight friends can be just as caring and supportive as your queer friends. So even if you don't have any LGBTQ+ friends yet (this will be a lot easier in college, if you go), find some straight folks who have your back and love you for who you are.

Finding a community is hard work, but it's essential. Just like any teen, but especially as an LGBTQ+ teen, you're going to be walking through some pretty heavy stuff in the next few years. You're making big life decisions, discovering more about who you are, stepping into your future! You'll face family issues, faith questions, relationship challenges, and a lot of other stuff.

But you don't need to face these challenges alone. In fact, you really shouldn't face them alone. We're not meant to function that way. Whoever you find, whoever finds you, be bold and intentional about creating your community. It may not be the amazing, artistic, advocating queer community you pictured at first. It may be small, shy, even in secret. But it's *your* community. And it's to be treasured.

★ IT WON'T ALWAYS BE LIKE THIS

Though you may feel alone now, know that you'll have far more opportunity to find your people in the future. It's a big colorful world out there, and your community is waiting for you! Engage, safely and earnestly, with the community you're in now. Leave it more loving, more accepting, and more queer than you found it. And look forward to college, career, or whatever opportunity comes next!

HELP! I'M IN LOVE WITH (OR AT LEAST CRUSHING HARD ON) MY BEST FRIEND!

Oh, crushes . . . they're exciting, aren't they? Well, exciting but also embarrassing and awkward and panic-inducing. *Especially* when it's your best friend!

Crushes happen all the time, in the straight and the queer world alike. They're perfectly natural and normal, and crushing on a friend is soooo common. You spend time together, share hobbies and interests, get to know each other's pasts, and share future dreams. You have a relationship—a friendly one—and it's natural that this might lead you to feeling something, well, *more* than friendly.

Admitting your feelings is never easy. We won't pretend otherwise. We also won't deny that being queer presents even more unique challenges to the whole "admitting crushes" thing. For instance, you're probably asking yourself a few extra questions, like:

* "Is my crush a lesbian (or gay or bi or trans-inclusive pansexual, etc.)?"

* "Does my crush know I am queer?"

* "Will admitting my feelings totally freak them out?"

* "Am I going to lose their friendship?"

There's no one right way to go about handling crushes. Some people bury them in the deep, dark pages of a diary until they fade into oblivion (or until one of you moves out of town after graduation). Some people choose to come clean and make it known. But even this can happen in countless ways. There's the grand romantic gesture or *Bachelorette*-style proposal (umm . . . probably not). There's the normal "between friends, I need to tell you something" conversation. There's the sheepish, stare-at-your-shoelaces-and-blurt-out-all-the-words-in-a-five-second-tornado admission. And so on.

★ THINGS TO CONSIDER

Before you do nothing, or something, or *everything*, take some time to think over a few questions. First, and most importantly: Are you out to this person? How did they respond when you came out to them? If you're not out to them, why not? Coming out to someone *and* telling them that you have feelings for them at the same time is a LOT.

Next, and not less important: What about your crush? Are *they* out? Do you have reason to believe this person is queer, or at least would not be completely stunned and surprised to hear about your feelings? They certainly don't *have* to be out for you to communicate how you feel. But there is a lot to consider in these matters. Like, who is your crush likely to process this with? Their mom? Are you okay being out to their mom?

These questions are not at the heart of your feelings, and they're not meant to scare you off (be BOLD, you beauty!). But you should at least think through your plan. And while you can't predict or control every factor of what response you might get, you can take a moment to turn down those endorphins (*soooo* hard to do) and think about things rationally. In fact, why don't you go ahead and pull out that notebook and make another pro/con list?

Some costs of saying something:

* This friendship might change for the worse. Or maybe, unfortunately, it could end. Life is full of risk.

* If you're not out already to your crush, you're letting another person in on the information, and it will be theirs to share (or, hopefully, not share, but you never know).

* If they're straight . . . well . . . we don't have to tell you how that would feel. Not great, that's for sure.

The benefits of saying something:

* You have been brave! And you've been true to yourself! No matter the response, just saying something is a major win!

* They might like you back! AHHHAHAHAHHHHHHHHHH, win-win!

* The friendship could change for the better! Even if it doesn't turn into a romantic relationship, your honesty and willingness to confide in a friend might strengthen the bonds of your friendship.

So . . . you've considered all the factors and . . . you want to say something. What do you do now?

★ HOW NOT TO TELL SOMEONE YOU LIKE THEM

"Confessing your feelings" to someone is never going to be perfect. And that's okay—it means you're a real person, not a character in a romantic comedy. But there are certainly some things that could ruin a healthy conversation with your crush. Here are two of the most important:

* Don't drop the "L" word. "I love you" or "I'm in love with you" might sound romantic and charming in movies, and maybe even in your head as you play out the scene. But in real life, *love* can be heavy, and serious, and scary. Odds are good that your feelings will change, and if they don't, you have plenty of time to share.

* Don't flirt forever. Some harmless flirting is fun and useful in discovering how someone feels about you. Do it and learn what you can. But then take action one way or another, because too much flirting can be awkward, even painful, for the other person, and/or for you. Be direct. Be proud of who you are. How you feel is how you feel! Don't be ashamed; speak your truth!

★ HOW TO TELL SOMEONE HOW YOU FEEL

There's no perfect rulebook for this stuff, and every situation is different. But we can't tell you what NOT to do without providing a few tips for making sure the convo goes as well as you hope.

* Plan what you want to say before the moment. Don't wing it. Trust us.

★ Be direct and honest, and avoid confusion. Say something like, "I like you, more than friends. And I just want to be honest with you about how I'm feeling." Avoid saying, "Hey, like, I think I might, like, so for a long time I've had this feeling, and well, I just, when I'm around you my chest, and, I don't know if you even, well, what I'm trying to say is, I think, unless you are not even into, okay. Hold on . . . ."

➧ Communicate that you are, first and foremost, their friend. Your friendship may change, but it doesn't have to stop because feelings have been expressed. Avoid giving ultimatums ("If you don't like me, then I don't think we can be friends."). This does not have to be the be-all-end-all conversation on which every second of the rest of your friendship depends. It might be that. But it doesn't have to be.

★ REJECTION—OH, HOW CRUEL

Cue the violins. Recite a melodramatic Shakespearean sonnet, cry into tissues, while eating all the chocolate soaked in tears.

Here's an obvious truth: Rejection sucks.

When your crush doesn't feel the same way as you or, even worse, doesn't want to be friends anymore, it can be painful. It can feel like your world has shattered. Especially if this is your first time telling a queer crush how you feel.

We promise your world hasn't ended. It's just changed. And in time, you'll see it has changed for the better.

Still, and we're not trying to be pessimistic here, but you should plan for rejection. In any given crush or dating situation, the odds are just better that the other person isn't going to feel it. And if you are ready for it, you can avoid that whole "spurned love" deal.

You're better than that! Your friendship deserves more than that. Rejection doesn't necessarily mean your friendship has to end. But you have to be kind, realistic, and mature in order to move forward. Set boundaries for your own heart, and respect the boundaries your friend needs as well. Don't take a rejection as a personal insult. Try not to assume that *no one is ever going to love me, ever!* They will. Honestly, they will.

Time is a great healer (other great healers: sad songs, puppy/kitty cuddles, long walks, tearjerker movies). Eventually, you'll move on, you'll fall for someone else, and maybe it will go better next time. Who knows. But along the way you'll learn oh-so-much about yourself and the kind of person you truly want to be with. So, have a good cry if you need to, but go to school the next day with your head high. You were honest and brave, and there's no crime in a crush.

Mimi, 23:

> Learn from my mistakes! Know your limits and resolve to respect boundaries. This goes for reciprocated and unreciprocated crushes, your personal boundaries, AND the boundaries of the other person. If your crush doesn't like you back, be respectful. Don't flirt with them. Don't put yourself in situations where you might be tempted to do something they don't want to do. This can be anything from being alone in a room or car with you, to acting on your physical desires toward them, and more. If your crush does like you back, be willing to have intentional (and sometimes hard) conversations with them about what having a crush means and doesn't mean.

HELP! I'M A HORNY QUEER TEENAGER!

And we've finally gotten to the sex part. What is there to say about being a horny queer teenager?

Well, first and foremost: Whatever you're feeling with regard to sex, it's normal (this includes if you're *not, ever*, thinking about sex. If that's you, skip this section and jump to page 151). Thinking about sex can be awkward and isolating, and that goes double for queer people, and triple for queer Christians. But please know you're not the first or only teenager (gay or straight) to want to have sex. Like, *really* want to have sex.

Sex is an important, and wonderful, and sacred, and *fun* part of life. In church, we don't talk about sex very much. And queer

sex? Almost never. And when sex does get talked about in church, often it's cloaked in shame and stigma and sin. It's a thing we are often told not to do, not to think about, not to "give in to."

If you belong to a church that treats sex in such a manner, well, that attitude is a failure of your church. There's a wise and healthy way to discuss sex, and we need to start engaging in that conversation. After all, straight or queer, sex is a topic you're going to confront over and over for the rest of your life.

★ WHAT ARE WE TALKING ABOUT WHEN WE TALK ABOUT "SEX"?

Let's just be clear. Talking about and thinking about and even obsessing about sex is not embarrassing, shameful, or wrong. Being open and frank about matters of sex is one of the great benefits offered by the queer community. We understand that sex is a matter of mutuality and negotiation (It kind of has to be, when you think about it. The basic assumptions of *who puts what where* just don't exist!).

In this book, like in life, *sex* means sex. All of it. Sex is not just the penetrative act of intercourse. That understanding of sex is inadequate. When we talk about sex, we're talking about *all* the stuff that happens with one's body for the purpose of sexual pleasure.

That includes intercourse, sure. But it's also everything else you do with a partner for pleasure. And it's what you do by yourself. Yep, masturbation is sex (based on the research, you're probably familiar with that subject already).

★ YOU ALWAYS HAVE OPTIONS

The simplest sex question is: *Should I have sex or not?*

The simplest answer is: *Maybe?* How's that for advice?

Look. If you don't want to have sex, for any reason—you're

waiting till graduation or marriage, you haven't found the right person, you're just plain not interested right now—that's okay! You certainly don't have to have sex now. You should never feel pressure from *anyone* to have sex, ever. You don't have to do anything you don't want to do, ever.

Being a teenager comes with loads of internal and external judgment. There's pressure to have sex, and pressure not to have sex. People who don't have sex get shamed for it, and people who do have sex get shamed for it. You can't win! Just ignore all of that—as best you can. If you're making your decision from a healthy, non-shameful place, stick to it. You know yourself, and you know what you want. It may change with time, and that's okay.

Eventually—whether it's in a week or several years from now—you'll likely decide to have sex. When you do, here are some things to remember.

★ SAFETY FIRST

Sorry to sound like your school's health teacher here, but this is soooooo important. Whether you want to have sex or are already doing so, we're just going to say a few things about safety. All three are an absolute must, now and forever, for queer people, straight people, all people:

1) **BE SAFE.**

1) **PRACTICE CONSENT.**

2) **USE PROTECTION.**

★ SAFE-SEX PRACTICES

In our society, most of what you will learn about safe sex is going to be about how to, and whether to, use contraception in opposite-sex sexual intercourse.

When thinking about safety and queer sex, it might seem like there's not a lot of good info out there for LGBTQ+ teens. But there is, if you know where to look and who to ask. Definitely check out the resources section at the back of the book, but for the basics, we're here to help! Because safe sex isn't only important for straight sex. And it definitely is not just about contraception. All sexual activity in all relationships should be safe, healthy, and fun. Those words might mean different things to different people, so always be clear with your partner.

> **QUICK DEFINITIONS**
>
> **consent:** expressed permission to do something, to be of the same mind or opinion.
>
> **safe sex:** sexual activity in which people try to protect themselves from sexual diseases, by using a condom, for example.

Practicing safe sex should be a conversation you and your partner have together. Make sure (before the heat of the moment) that both you and your partner are using protection. Here are the high-level, super-important considerations for safe, fun, mutually satisfying queer sex:

- ✦ Contraception, including condoms.
- ✦ Birth control.
- ✦ Lubricant. (If the idea of stopping the heat to re-lube mid-sex embarrasses you so much that you aren't willing to buy lube, you're not ready for sex.)
- ✦ Medications. Talk to your doctor (or Planned Parenthood) about pre-exposure prophylaxis (PrEP) or post-exposure prophylaxis (PEP).
- ✦ Vaccinations.

★ Conversations. Don't make assumptions about what sex will look like. When the time comes, you will both be glad you talked about it beforehand (trust us!).

★ This is always important, but we want to make a special note: If you or your partner are transgender or genderqueer, be specific. Never assume you know what someone else will enjoy during sex.

Obviously not all of these apply to every sexual situation. But every one that does *needs* to be addressed thoughtfully.

★ SAFE-SEX MYTHS

★ "It kills the vibe." It doesn't. Especially if you and your partner have already had the conversation. Whatever "it" is (condom, lube, anything), you're still going to want to have sex with this person after you take care of it!

★ "Protection makes sex less enjoyable." If anything, sex is more enjoyable when practiced safely. Practicing safe sex means less anxiety during and after sex.

★ "I'll be able to tell if someone has herpes. Or chlamydia. Or whatever." Probably not. Many sexually transmitted infections (STIs) don't have visible symptoms all the time. But they're often still contagious.

★ "Condoms don't work anyway." Condoms work 98 percent of the time. 98 PERCENT! Don't use this line, and if someone uses it on you, be very wary.

★ "Oral/Anal sex is safer than vaginal sex." Not really. Safer is a tricky word and one that you should be wary of. All forms of sex come with risk.

HIV. Anyone who participates in any kind of unprotected sex faces a risk of HIV. And for gay and bisexual men, the risks are higher. Regardless of what kind of sex you are having, it's important to know the facts and work against the stigma that has been attached to HIV.

HIV = Human immunodeficiency virus. It's transmitted through the blood or semen of an HIV-positive person. About 1.1 million Americans are living with HIV, and about 15% of those people do not know they have it. It's crucial to get tested.

Today, there are highly effective drugs to protect people from HIV. They are PrEP and PEP.

PrEP is an HIV prevention drug that, when taken daily, has been shown to be 99% effective at stopping the transmission of HIV during sex. PEP is a drug administered after potential exposure with HIV. It must be started within 72 hours of exposure.

These drugs are highly effective, and it is important to know where you can get them. But the best protection against HIV is still condoms. Use condoms for any form of penetrative sex (this includes oral sex!).

★ NO MEANS NO. EVERY. SINGLE. TIME.

Any and all sexual activity requires clear consent. Without consent, sex is not sex—it's assault. And while you probably know this, you also probably know that assault still happens. A lot. It's absolutely crucial to understand consent: it will keep you safe, and it will make every sexual experience more pleasurable.

Consent is mutual. Consent is not a one-time question. It's not a flippant, "You're good with this, right?" Consent is a conversation that occurs before, during, and after any sexual activity. Consent should be given by both partners equally. Consent can change at any moment when one person is suddenly uncomfortable or doesn't want to continue. Consent cannot be given when one person is drunk or high. Consent should be given before any and all sexual activity. This includes kissing, touching, removing clothes, and everything thereafter. Make sure you and your partner are okay with what activity is going on.

Consent should *always be respected*. Know that you have a right, at any time, to say, "Stop," or "I'm not comfortable with that." You're not being selfish or hypocritical. You are respecting yourself and your boundaries, as you should! Your partner deserves this same respect. We know it's hard when the

---

What is sexual assault? RAINN defines sexual assault as behavior that occurs without explicit consent of the victim. It includes:

- Unwanted sexual touching
- Forcing sexual acts, such as oral sex
- Emotionally or psychologically manipulating another into sexual acts
- Attempted rape
- Rape

Sexual assault is never the fault of the victim. If you are the victim of sexual assault and are unsure what to do next, call the National Sexual Assault Hotline: 800-656-HOPE.

---

hormones are raging, but if your partner, at any point, does not give consent for an activity, stop immediately. (Of course, we're assuming you asked for consent at the beginning, too.)

We cannot state this firmly enough. *Without consent, all sexual behavior (not just penetration) is assault.*

★ APPS AND SOCIAL MEDIA

Sex today is tangled up in dating and hookup apps, and knowing how to navigate these spaces safely is crucial to having safe sex. Most dating and hookup apps require that you be eighteen before joining. Please, friends, adhere to this. We're not saying this to be killjoys. We know that online dating can be a wonderful and safe experience for lots of queer people. But we also promised to be real with you. And the truth is that there are a lot of dangerous, creepy people out there who can and do take advantage of others. Some of  those dangerous people target youth; others target queer youth who are looking for connection and support.

We want you to be safe and empowered. We want you to avoid being taken advantage of by strangers or predators. Online dating or hookup sites can look and sound legitimate. But on these sites, it can be easy to get caught up in the moment or tricked by a predator (which is not your fault, but be aware that it does happen).

For as long as you can, please avoid the apps. Never give personal information to anyone you don't know online. Never send pictures on the apps or meet anyone from the apps in a private place. Just don't use them.

⭐ IT'S MY FIRST TIME . . . HELP!

This is a safe space, and we're not here to tell you whether or when to have sex. We're here to help you live your best queer life. So whether it happens this year or in ten years, let's go ahead and discuss your first time.

Having sex for the first time is a big decision. It's not, like, a life-altering, panic-inducing, irrevocably big decision that defines everything about what your future will look like (despite what you may have heard). We don't want you to be terrified. But when, how, and who you have sex with for the first time are important things to think about.

WHAT NOT TO DO:

* ⭐ Never meet up with anyone you don't know. (That is, don't hook up with a stranger for your first time.) It may seem like a low-risk way to "test the waters." It's not. It's potentially dangerous, and it's just not a very satisfying way to start your sex life. Make your first time special; make it with someone you care about.

* ⭐ Don't have sex because you feel pressured to follow through. You may have decided, "Yes! Tonight is the night! I'm gonna do it!"—only to feel hesitation, discomfort, or disinterest in the moment. That's okay. Don't follow through with a decision just for the sake of expectation or pressure. Remember, you can say no at *any time.*

* ⭐ Don't trust the other person to come prepared. Of course, *ideally* they will. You will have, hopefully, talked about sex at least enough to *both* be prepared. But you should also have your own protection, condoms, lube, etc. Your sexual health is *your* responsibility.

- ★ Don't do drugs or drink beforehand. Few, if any, good decisions about sex have resulted under the influence. Stay sober for this!

WHAT TO DO:

- ★ Use protection and get/give consent. (Are you getting the message here, or . . . ?).

- ★ Meet up in public first, even if it's not the first time you've met. Let a trusted friend know where you are, where you're going, and how they can contact you (and know how you can contact them).

- ★ Trust your intuition. If it feels wrong at any moment, if you're uncomfortable, or if you just change your mind and want to stop, try to say something, if you can put your feelings into words. If not, know it's always okay to leave.

- ★ Have fun! Learn about yourself. It's okay if it's awkward. You're allowed to laugh! You don't have to pretend to be an expert.

★ LAST THOUGHT

Safe, consensual, queer, wonderful sex is a beautiful part of life and relationships. But it's not something to be jumped into the moment the act falls into your lap (so to speak). Consent and protection are how you honor yourself and your partner as you explore a new dynamic of your relationship.

Sex done well takes responsibility and thoughtfulness. Accept your responsibility to practice sex safely, use protection, and put consent first. If you're not willing to do those things, then you're not ready for sex yet. Sorry. But that's just the truth.

INTERLUDE:

The ABCs of LGBTQ+ Cultural Icons

Getting you started with twenty-six fabulous figures and organizations for you to find. These twenty-six people, some who you might already know, and some might be new to you—will start your exploration of modern queer culture.

A: ACT UP – AIDS Coalition to Unleash Power, founded in 1987 during the AIDS epidemic.

B: JAMES BALDWIN – gay novelist, playwright, activist, cultural giant.

C: MARGARET CHO – bisexual comedian, actor, burlesque performer, human rights activist.

D: JAMES DEAN – the bisexual actor, who died tragically at twenty-four, left a legacy that's impossible to overstate.

E: ELSA – the Queen of Arendelle, queen of our queer hearts, helped lots of young queer people "Let It Go" (can't hold it back anymore).

F: MICHEL FOUCAULT – postmodern French philosopher and historian. You'll probably be assigned to read him in college (do it).

G: JUDY GARLAND – Dorothy from *The Wizard of Oz*, and the ultimate Gay Icon of the twentieth century.

H: LANGSTON HUGHES – poet and central figure in the Harlem Renaissance. Hughes's sexuality is debated, but his status as an icon in the community is beyond debate.

I: DANA INTERNATIONAL – Israeli pop singer and transgender woman who won the Eurovision Song Contest in 1998 (that's a big deal!).

J: ELTON JOHN – flamboyant singer, AIDS activist, icon.

K: FRIDA KAHLO – Mexican painter and feminist whose work dealt with indigenous history, politics, and queerness.

L: AUDRE LORDE – lesbian writer, poet, feminist, womanist, civil rights activist. Her work was an early vision of intersectionality.

M: HARVEY MILK – the first openly gay politician elected in California. His assassination in 1978 led to national outrage and riots in San Francisco.

N: CHANI NICHOLAS – queer astrologist who uses astrology as a lens for understanding feminism, politics, and justice. In doing so, she's become a source of hope and meaning for queer and trans people.

O: FRANK OCEAN – singer, rapper, photographer. Ocean's bisexual coming-out letter made international headlines and cemented his iconic status.

P: BILLY PORTER – Broadway and television actor, fashion god.

Q: NITZA ILEANA QUIÑONES ALEJANDRO – first Latinx lesbian appointed to serve as US federal judge.

R: RuPAUL – drag queen, actor, activist, singer, model, and a media titan. *RuPaul's Drag Race* has brought drag into the mainstream.

S: MATTHEW SHEPARD – gay university student whose murder in 1998 became an international media story and flashpoint for hate-crime protections for LGBTQ+ people. The Matthew Shepard and James Byrd Jr. Hate Crimes Prevention Act was signed in 2008.

T: ALAN TURING – British mathematician, computer scientist, and genius who worked as a Nazi code breaker before being arrested and castrated for being gay. In 2013, the British government "apologized."

U: URSULA – from *The Little Mermaid*. Inspired in look and attitude by drag queen Divine, Ursula has achieved queer/drag goddess status.

V: JONATHAN VAN NESS – nonbinary hair-dresser who became an International Icon for All Queers Everywhere with his role in *Queer Eye*.

W: LILLY AND LANA WACHOWSKI – transgender sisters and filmmakers behind the *Matrix* series.

X: LIL NAS X – rapper and trailblazer whose country rap song "Old Town Road" was a viral sensation. He's the only LGBTQ+ artist to ever win a Country Music Award.

Y: BOWEN YANG – comedian and actor, first Chinese American cast member on *Saturday Night Live* (and third gay man on the show).

Z: ZINES – uncompromising, self-published, cheaply produced magazines that were vital to the early LGBTQ+ rights movement. A powerful source of queer activist strategy, art, and inspiration for decades of queer people.

This list goes on and on, forever. Keep searching for your own inspiration.

IS BULLYING DEFINITELY GOING TO HAPPEN TO ME? WHAT SHOULD I DO ABOUT IT?

"Bullying" and "LGBTQ+" may seem like synonymous terms to you (they certainly will to parents and family). That's because, as many understand things, being bullied is just a part of being queer, right? Just one of those things we have to put up with. *shrug* *sigh*

It's easy to think that. And depending on your own circumstances, you may already have experienced bullying in school, church, or maybe even from adults or family members at home. If so, you may feel like there's no escape from bullying. This is false, and it's the kind of thinking that is easy to succumb to when we forget that we belong to the most kick-ass club in the world: the fabulous queer community.

Bullying can happen almost anywhere and in many different ways. And while bullying is a problem for straight and queer teens, being LGBTQ+ might lead you to experience bullying more than others.

★ THE NUMBERS

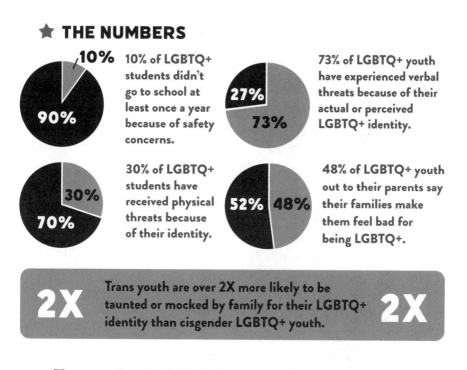

10% of LGBTQ+ students didn't go to school at least once a year because of safety concerns.

73% of LGBTQ+ youth have experienced verbal threats because of their actual or perceived LGBTQ+ identity.

30% of LGBTQ+ students have received physical threats because of their identity.

48% of LGBTQ+ youth out to their parents say their families make them feel bad for being LGBTQ+.

2X Trans youth are over 2X more likely to be taunted or mocked by family for their LGBTQ+ identity than cisgender LGBTQ+ youth. **2X**

These numbers look bleak. But as we talk about bullying and how you can respond to it, we want you to know one thing: *Bullying is never your fault. NEVER.*

★ IF YOU ARE BEING BULLIED

You are not to blame for the actions of anyone who bullies you. Whether it's by classmates or siblings or parents, you're being bullied because of *them*. Often that person has experienced trauma or feels some kind of deep pain, and they are taking it out on you. Sometimes that person is just mean. Either way, we're so sorry.

Bullying is a terrible thing to endure. Never think that "changing" your identity is the right solution to make bullying stop. At the heart of the matter, you're not being bullied because you're queer. Bullying is always the bully's fault, and the fault of anyone who fails to protect people from bullies. It's never your fault.

We're not talking about bullying in order to scare you, but to help you feel prepared for what may happen (or to help you deal with what already has happened). If reading about bullying is too hard, it's okay to skip ahead. You can also read or talk through this section with a friend. It may help to have another person for support as you think about what you read.

★ NO MORE EXCUSES

Like we said earlier, bullying can happen in so many different forms. This can sometimes make bullying hard to recognize. Even when you know you're being bullied, it can be hard to admit it to yourself, let alone to others. Maybe you feel like you deserve it (you don't), or that telling someone will only make it worse.

These are the excuses we make to justify inaction. There is no excuse for bullying. Ever. No one deserves to be bullied. Everyone has the right to speak up. We know that's scary, but we're going to give you some practical tools to help you take on bullying in a safe way.

If you are not being bullied, it's still crucially important to understand what it is, and to know the tools to intervene on behalf of those who might need it.

★ TYPES OF BULLYING

We can't describe every type of bullying you might encounter. But there are four common types that you'll likely recognize: verbal, social, physical, and cyberbullying. Here are some examples of each. (This information and much more can be found at stopbullying.gov.)

Verbal bullying is saying or writing unkind or unwelcome things. This includes:

* ★ teasing.
* ★ name-calling or intentionally misusing names/pronouns.
* ★ inappropriate or unwanted sexual comments.
* ★ taunting.
* ★ threatening to harm you in any way.

Social bullying involves harming someone's relationships, friendships, or reputation. This includes:

* ★ excluding someone on purpose.
* ★ telling classmates or other peers to ignore or mistreat someone.
* ★ spreading rumors and gossip about someone.
* ★ embarrassing or outing someone in public.

Physical bullying involves hurting a person or their possessions. This includes:

* ★ hitting/kicking/punching.
* ★ spitting.
* ★ tripping/pushing.
* ★ stealing, hiding, or destroying someone's things.
* ★ making mean or rude hand gestures.

Cyberbullying is any type of bullying that takes place over digital devices, laptops, cell phones, etc. This includes:

* ★ taunting, teasing, name-calling, etc. through texting, email, or direct messaging.

- public embarrassment or humiliation of someone on social media sites, or anywhere online.
- sharing pictures or information without permission.
- threatening physical harm online.
- pushing someone to suicidal thoughts or actions through any online communication.

Cyberbullying presents some unique challenges that traditional bullying doesn't:

PERSISTENT: Cyberbullying can feel impossible to escape. If a bully is constantly texting or messaging you, it can be difficult to find relief.

PERMANENT: Information, pictures, anything communicated electronically is very hard to erase, if it's not quickly reported and removed. A negative online reputation, including for those who bully, can impact college admissions, employment, and other areas of life.

HARD TO NOTICE: If you don't say something about experiencing cyberbullying, no one else may notice that it's happening. Teachers, parents, or your friends may not overhear or see cyberbullying taking place.

★ HOW TO RESPOND TO BULLYING

Now that we've explained some different forms of bullying, let's talk about what you can do. You are not powerless! You can and should take action against bullying, whether it's happening to you or you see it happening to others.

Before you can respond to bullying, you need to admit that it's happening. If you see it happening to someone else, in as kind a manner as you can, help them understand the same. It sounds simple, but it can be hard. If you've made excuses for the person bullying you, explained away their behavior, or told yourself, "It's not really that bad," it's time to stop. If someone is making you or others feel uncomfortable or afraid for any reason, their actions are not okay. And they need to be reported.

Speaking out about bullying can be scary. What if reporting something only makes it worse? What if others won't believe you? Or, worse, what if they take the other person's side? These are scary questions because sometimes these things do happen. But more often than not, reporting bullying will lead to intervention and a safer environment for everyone (it's highly unlikely a bully only targets one person). Either way, we want you to be prepared to report bullying in the best way possible.

+ **BE SPECIFIC.** When you experience or witness bullying, write down when and where it happened, who was involved, who else witnessed it, and what actions occurred.

+ **BRING THE RECEIPTS.** If this is cyberbullying, screenshot everything. Keep the texts and messages long enough to show the proper authorities. If this was an in-person case of bullying, take along a witness who was there. If no one else witnessed the act except you and the person who bullied, you should still report the incident.

+ **GO TO THE RIGHT PERSON.** Telling your parents is a good, safe first step (because, hopefully, they're going to have your back and go to the mat for you!). Beyond that, identify who the next person you should tell is. If bullying occurred at school, report to a counselor or the principal. If it occurred at church, talk to your youth pastor or another trusted leader.

- **LEAN ON YOUR PEOPLE.** You don't have to report bullying alone. You may absolutely bring anyone with you who makes you feel safe, strong, and secure.

- **INVOLVE THE AUTHORITIES WHEN APPROPRIATE.** Bullying and cyberbullying can be illegal, and sometimes law enforcement needs to be involved. If someone is threatening physical harm, committing acts of vandalism, stalking, blackmailing, or urging self-harm or suicide, report them to the police. Before reaching out to authorities, ask a trusted adult or parent to go with you. If the bullying is targeted specifically at your queerness, this means you are being harassed, and that is illegal.

★ YOU'VE REPORTED THE BULLYING . . . NOW WHAT?

Sometimes when you report bullying, it stops altogether. The person might be removed from whatever physical space presents the opportunity, limiting their chances to interact with a victim. But this might take a while . . . or it might not happen at all. No matter what action the authorities and the other person take, you still have a say in your own treatment. You can take action. Advocate for yourself and for the safety of everyone (these are the same thing!).

★ OUT OF THERE

If you're encountering bullying somewhere, *leave that space.* We know this is often easier said than done. How are you supposed to leave school? Or your church? Or, God forbid, your family?? These are some of the hardest questions faced by queer teens, but that doesn't mean they don't need to be asked.

Discuss these questions with a safe, affirming resource: a counselor, a therapist, or, if it's not a home-based issue, your parents. See what your options are. Maybe it's a simple classroom move, or maybe it's a bigger solution (moving schools or even moving out). Whatever the solutions may be, they'll require emotional and practical support from others. This can feel exhausting, especially if you're still encountering the bullying. Keep pushing! Remember that you are perfect and loved, and you deserve a safe and secure life.

Finding a solution can bring freedom and healing in the long run, even if it's a little more work right now.

★ WHEN YOU HAVE TO STAY

If you can't leave the space, you can still set up boundaries. Find ways to limit your interactions with negative, harmful people. Block them from your phone and from all social media. Don't engage with them verbally or physically when you see them. If they provoke you, respond calmly and inform them who you'll report them to. Again, all of this is easier said than done. Waiting it out until graduation is not a good idea at all (unless you're a senior nearing graduation). Ignoring the problem isn't going to make it go away. Take what actions you can to protect yourself and others.

★ SELF-CARE YOUR WAY THROUGH

Self-care is always important, and it's *especially* important when you're undergoing bullying. Give yourself space to grieve, punch pillows, or scream at the universe. It's okay to be upset and angry. Bullying sucks! Self-care can help you rebuild after the trauma from bullying.

It's okay to indulge in your personal delights as part of self-care, be it a bubble bath, ice cream, or boxing classes (we don't know, but you do). But self-care also means taking care of your heart and your emotions. Be intentional about this. Surround yourself with affirming, encouraging voices. Whether it's friends, family, or an uplifting YouTuber, find something that fills you up again. For every negative voice in your life, listen to three that build you up. Fight back with truth, and choose not to believe the lies and negative voices of those who are bullying.

And don't forget one of the best tools in the queer self-care tool kit: see a therapist. Therapists and counselors can be a tremendous help when you're processing bullying. Therapists provide a safe space for you to express how you're feeling and work through trauma. Remember that there is always a serious level of confidentiality between therapists and their clients. What you share is not going to become gossip.

★ YOU'RE NOT ALONE

Bullies succeed by isolating their targets, making them feel alone and cut off from help. If you're being bullied or you witness bullying, be intentional about finding love and support. Lean on others when you're weak. Cry with them when you're angry. Fight back with them with grace and courage. If you see someone else being bullied, support them in the same way. Make sure they know they aren't alone either.

You are a strong, beautiful, resilient member of our beloved queer community. And while it's sad to say, part of what makes us strong, beautiful, and resilient is our ability to persevere. Know that others have made it through exactly what you're facing now. Time *will* bring you through this, heal your heart, and move you on to a new, hopefully safer space.

★ LAST THOUGHT

Often, bullying goes unreported because we think it's "not bad enough" to be called out. We want to assure you that all bullying absolutely *is* bad enough, because you deserve a happy, healthy, and safe life, everywhere, all the time.

Don't let bullying slide. Leave the environment and report the person. Surround yourself with allies. And *always* take care of yourself and others.

WHAT IF MY FRIENDS REJECT ME?

Rejection may be one of your biggest fears about being queer. Fear of rejection is at the root of what keeps us in the closet. What happens when we're out? Who will reject us? And is coming out, in the end, worth it?

After you come out, that fear might become real. It's true. Many times coming out leads directly to rejection. If you haven't yet, you probably will experience some form of rejection. And we're sorry. Rejection is just the worst.

But you know what? It's their loss.

We know that sounds like something a mom would say. But seriously, hear us out.

★ THE TRUTH ABOUT REJECTION

Rejection can come in many forms after someone comes out as LGBTQ+. Among the most common forms are being ignored or alienated by peers, being told by "friends" that your queerness is wrong or sinful, being abandoned by close friends, bullying, mocking, or receiving homophobic or transphobic comments.

When these things come from the people we thought cared for us, it can be devastating. But when someone rejects you because of your gender identity or sexual orientation, the truth is this:

★ YOU ARE BETTER OFF WITHOUT THEM

Friends express differences all the time. And your friends, at school or church or wherever, will each have their own individual response to the fact of your queerness. But rejection should not be among those responses.

Our loved ones—even those who might "disagree" with being queer—should still be able to celebrate and support who we are. Being LGBTQ+ is a wonderful gift. Disagreeing with that statement is *not cause for rejection*. So, if one of your friends rejects you because they don't "agree" with or "condone" who you are, they are not a healthy presence in your life.

Of course, realizing that the person you thought was a friend suddenly isn't, doesn't really feel great, right? Losing a friend can be extremely painful! You may feel disoriented, confused, angry. That's okay; that's normal. You've been hurt.

★ TIME HEALS

If you've been rejected by someone you care about, it's okay to be angry or hurt. It's okay to grieve the loss, because our social relationships are extremely important. Anger and sadness don't mean you're doing something wrong. You may need to take some time and just be *upset*. Those emotions are essential phases of healing and moving on.

And yes, we know you don't want to hear this—no one ever does—but often, time is the best (and only) healer. Eventually, the intensity of your pain will soften. You will find new friends, your heart will heal, and you'll be stronger because of the difficulties you've experienced. Don't let the rejection of others stop you from stepping into who you are.

Be proud of your queerness, and let those who can't support you go. Those people are toxic to the queer experience, and they will not be allies to you as you discover your fully authentic and fabulous self.

★ HOW TO FIND COMMUNITY

We hope you never face real rejection, but even if you do, know that there are people out there who will *not* reject you, who will accept you for exactly who you are. There are so many welcoming communities you can be a part of. There are affirming churches and sports leagues and social groups and online spaces and schools. And there are other queer people, so many of us, just waiting to find and love you.

One day, you'll be able to surround yourself with what queer people often call your chosen family—those people, queer or not, blood family or not, that you intentionally choose to be closest to. Until then, spend time with safe, trustworthy friends. Find a welcoming online community that will listen to and support you. Rejection is another person's choice, but you can combat the feeling of isolation that you might feel as a result. Be brave and keep trying to make connections.

★ REJECTION IS NOT ALWAYS PERMANENT

Many times, when we are rejected by our friends, they come around to see just how glorious our queerness is. It's very common for strained relationships to heal in time, be it in days, months, or years. People change, and one way we love others is by respecting that change.

Now, that doesn't mean we have to forgive and forget. Sometimes rejection comes with lasting trauma or harm. Letting the people who caused that hurt back into our lives is risky. But if your ex-friends have a change of heart, be open to hearing them out. Rejection is terrible. But reconciliation can be beautiful.

Asa, 23:

If there is anything I have learned in the almost-two-years since I came out, it's that everyone has a place in the "queer world." Sure, some people are more visible and accepted. White cisgender gay people are still an unfortunately dominant voice, and even among the more marginalized groups there are still unnecessary hierarchies. But the best part of being part of the queer world is that you can finally find someone like you. No matter who you are attracted to, no matter what your gender is, and no matter what you look like, there is probably someone in the same boat. Even if you aren't interacting with someone who has the same pronouns, who dates people of the same gender or genders that you do, or who presents differently from you, the shared experience of not being cisgender or straight unites us all.

WHAT ABOUT THE BATHROOM?

Bathrooms. If you are gay, lesbian, bi, pan, or are out in any identity that includes same-gender attraction, bathrooms can be awkward or uncomfortable in your teenage years. If you're genderqueer, trans, or nonbinary, going to the bathroom might even feel dangerous. We'll call all of these feelings "The Bathroom Question," because it really is just one big ?????????.

If you are comfortable being out and using the bathroom, hold your head high and pee with pride! But if you feel anxious or uncomfortable answering the bathroom question, you're not alone!

 51% of trans youth were required to use restrooms that did not align with their gender.

 63% of trans students avoided using the bathroom at school all day.

These stats are about trans or gender-nonconforming students. But the bathroom question affects all LGBTQ+ students. Homophobic responses to queer people are all too common in our society. And it's not just in bathrooms. It's also locker rooms, shower facilities, health classes. Any space that is designed specifically to divide people into binary gender categories can be tricky for queer people.

★ IT'S NOT "SPECIAL TREATMENT"

Here's the baseline expectation for all students, queer or not: You should have access to bathrooms and locker rooms that make you feel safe and comfortable. Allowing all students to feel safe and comfortable is *not* special treatment.

If you're feeling uncomfortable with the bathroom situation at your school, you can say something! You have a right to ask for a safe bathroom!

What makes you feel comfortable is a separate question, and it's one you should spend some time thinking about. Do you want to use the bathroom that reflects your gender? Do you want gender-neutral spaces? It will benefit you to have an idea for a solution before you start the conversation.

The bathroom question matters. Providing facilities so everyone can pee in peace should be the baseline expectation of schools, churches, and *everywhere!* It's a matter of equality, safety, and social acceptance. Don't be ashamed or embarrassed to address this issue. Every queer person who comes after you will be grateful that you did.

★ SO . . . WHAT CAN I DO?

If you're ready to take action and confront the bathroom question, here are a few steps you can take.

> ✷ Find out if your school has a Gender Support Plan.

A Gender Support Plan is an incredibly useful tool for protecting LGBTQ+ students on your campus. A Gender Support Plan is usually a collaboration between school leaders, queer and transgender students, and their families. Gender Support Plans specifically address the issues that students like you may face at school, including bathrooms.

> ✷ If your school has a Gender Support Plan (GSP), read it!

Ask a teacher or administrator for a copy. Is there *any* policy about bathroom use? Are there policies that aren't being enforced? Knowing what your policies are can help you fight for your rights. If anyone (teachers, students, other parents) tries to force you to use a different restroom, pull out that GSP and wave it in their face! Okay, maybe don't do that. But don't be afraid to stand up for yourself, especially if you've got policy at your back!

> ✷ If your school doesn't have a Gender Support Plan, advocate for one.

If your school has no outlined policy on bathrooms/locker rooms, recommend that they create one immediately. Point out the benefits to the school from having such a policy, like student safety and legal accountability. If you have supportive parents, teachers, or a friend, take them with you. The more advocates for all-gender-friendly bathrooms, the better!

This is the kind of advocacy work that LGBTQ+ youth are especially effective at. You can ask for changes at your school better than adults because it is your issue, not ours. Doing so doesn't just help you; it helps every queer kid who comes after you.

★ WHAT IF NO ONE WILL LISTEN?

So, worst-case scenario: Your school has policies actively excluding transgender or gender-nonconforming students. You've advocated for a GSP. You've reported times you've felt unsafe or even been bullied. And still . . . no . . . change. No matter what, sometime or another, you're going to *have* to use a bathroom.

This is frustrating. Infuriating. Unfair. It's okay, you can be upset! Your school is letting you down. The administration of your school absolutely should be creating a safe environment *for you*. But if they aren't, if you're feeling unsafe and they still refuse? It might be time to consider other options.

If your parents are affirming and support your gender expression, talk about the challenges and ask what options exist. Can you transfer? Will they help you create an upswell of support for change in your school? You won't know if you don't ask.

If your parents are not affirming, or simply won't allow you to leave your school, we're sorry. You might have to stick it out. If you have to stick it out at school and just avoid the restroom all day, you certainly can. Plenty of LGBTQ+ teens do. But this isn't safe. Avoiding the bathroom regularly and for long stretches of time can cause urinary tract infections and even kidney damage. So if you are absolutely stuck, consider when and where you will be able to pee. Maybe the nurse's office during lunch? The locker room when it's empty? It's terrible that you even have to think this way, but healthy choices might exist even in bad situations.

★ BATHROOM BUDDIES

Look. We know the idea of a bathroom buddy is a bit childish. Don't use the phrase in the real world, maybe. But a bathroom buddy is about support, safety, and community. We all need those things.

So if you want a bathroom buddy, pick someone who is a strong, trustworthy ally, who is willing to stand up for you when you need it, and who knows what's at stake with the bathroom question. They can have your back and keep an eye out for bullying. They can help you advocate for a Gender Support Plan or some other bathroom policy. Or they can just pee. Whatever the case may be.

★ KNOW YOUR LIMITS

Remember, it's not your responsibility to create a safe space. The adults *should* be doing that for you. You are a minor under the protection of your school. You can advocate for yourself, but just like all our advice in this book, you do not *have* to. At the end of the day, you don't have to fight a policy battle if it makes you feel exposed, unsafe, or at risk.

★ LAST THOUGHT

The more you speak up and advocate for change, the more schools will start realizing the importance of including LGBTQ+ students in policy discussions. Remember, you're asking for *equal* treatment, not "special treatment."

WHAT ABOUT BEING QUEER ONLINE?

Hey. Put your phone down for a second so we can talk about the internet.

Our lives are lived online as much as (if not more than) they are at school, home, or church. For LGBTQ+ people in particular, the internet can be a place of community, support, and exploration. This is beautiful! But the internet also comes with risk.

★ LET'S TALK ABOUT THE GOOD FIRST!

We're sure you know this, but the internet is full of some of the most incredible, beautiful, supportive queer voices! When you're facing questions, harassment, or rejection from "real-life" people, your online community might be the first place you turn. Lots of people come out to their online community long before they do offline.

- ★ 73% of LGBTQ+ youth are more honest about themselves online than in the real world.
- ★ 50% of LGBTQ+ youth have at least one close friend online compared to 19% of their straight peers who have a close friend online.

✦ 66% of LGBTQ+ youth used the internet to connect with their LGBTQ+ community.

The internet is home to some of the most inspiring voices in the queer community. There are too many to name here, but you can find them on YouTube, Tumblr, Instagram, and the rest of your favorite online haunts.

Among those voices are many queer Christian advocates. Check out forums like Queer Grace Fellowship, Queer Theology, or Q Christian if you're looking for an encouraging, faithful community.

The internet also offers needed support for those in crisis. There are many online resources that can help LGBTQ+ teens, whatever kind of struggle may be coming up. In fact, over three-quarters of LGBTQ+ youth preferred to reach out for help online when they needed it. Asking for help online can feel safer, quicker, and more private than speaking to someone IRL.

Below is a selection of reliable online resources that you should be aware of.

- ★ **LGBT National Help Center: glbthotline.org/talkline**
- ★ **Trevor Project: thetrevorproject.org/get-help-now**

* **National Suicide Prevention Lifeline:** suicidepreventionlifeline.org/talk-to-someone-now
* **National Runaway Safeline:** 1800runaway.org
* **Crisis Text Line: Text "HOME" to 741741**

Take another look at those names, please. Knowing where to go for fast, queer supportive help in a crisis is extremely important. Not just for yourself, but for others in your life who may find themselves in need at any moment.

★ AND THE NOT-SO-GREAT SIDE . . .

So, yes, the internet can be a great place! But (big surprise coming . . .) it's got its dark side. There are a lot of voices out there who only want to tear you down or deceive you. And a lot of those voices sound wise and caring (they are neither). Many come from Christians who think they want to help (they are not helpful). Be smart, be discerning, and look out for online garbage.

Here are a few things to be aware of when you're scrolling through your newsfeed:

* **Misinformation**

  The internet isn't always the most reliable source of information (shock, right?). When you're seeking answers online, be wise. Start with well-known, affirming queer resources. Avoid blogs or websites that seem sketchy from the get-go. And if something sounds off, look for the same info elsewhere. It may sound boring to fact-check everything, but it's actually a responsible, mature way to engage online.

  Note: Any site that recommends or even suggests that conversion therapy works is spreading misinformation.

✴ Bullying/Cyberbullying

We talked about this earlier, but it's worth repeating. Cyberbullying is a very real and growing problem. In fact, the internet was one of the top three places that LGBTQ+ youth reported hearing negative messages. Social media, online forums, etc. are popular spaces for cyberbullying to take place. Be aware, and set boundaries to protect yourself from cyberbullying (more on boundaries later).

✴ False Self (or Catfishing)

It's easy to create a false self on the internet. It's easy for you, and it's easy for everyone else too. Being anonymous online is freeing and useful. It's a way to explore our queerness without the world watching over us. But if you ever get to the point where your online and real-life selves are quite literally two different people, please stop. That is dangerous territory. Rarely do we behave at our best when we're not being held accountable, and we don't want you to do anything you might regret, or that might have lasting consequences if your anonymity is revealed.

And, of course, that anonymity works the same way with everyone else in the whole world. Make friends and build your queer online community. You'll get years of value and support out of those people. But be smart and use common sense. You never know who's sitting IRL at the other computer. If anyone asks for money or other kinds of financial support, consider it a big red flag.

✴ Trolling

Trolling is a bit different than bullying. Online bullying usually comes from someone who you either know, or who knows you, offline. That is not how trolling works. Internet trolls attack whoever and whatever they want to, regardless of whether they know the people they're attacking. They stir up arguments, say hurtful things, and are all around just the worst. Their only purpose is to cause harm, and there are lots of anti-queer trolls on the internet. So look out for trolls, and for goodness' sake, PLEASE do not ever become one.

These are just some of the things to look out for online. In the next section, we'll talk a little more in-depth about how you can be safe and smart online, while still having fun!

HOW SHOULD I BE QUEER . . . ONLINE?

When it comes to the internet, we have one central piece of advice: get comfortable setting boundaries. It's an important part of being a person, and the better you are at setting boundaries, the more enjoyable your relationships (romantic, friendly, professional) will be.

So, yeah, the word *boundaries* probably doesn't inspire a lot of excitement in you. But we promise, you will be grateful (SO, *SO* GRATEFUL) in your future for learning how to set and stick to clear boundaries.

There's no better (or more important) place to learn how to do that than with online boundaries.

★ WHY WE NEED TO SET BOUNDARIES

Internet boundaries aren't just stupid rules to take away your fun. Having online boundaries is crazy important for a couple reasons:

★The internet is forever.

Such a warning is commonplace in media and classrooms. And it's (pretty much) true! Pictures, information, posts—once published, they are out there for anyone (and we mean *anyone*) to see. This may not seem so bad right now. But one day (and one day soon) you'll have college admissions or future employers scrolling through those tweets. So, even now, think before you "speak" online.

✦Anonymity isn't always foolproof.

The internet can feel like a super-safe place to hide. Well, it's not. Of course, there are levels of privacy and anonymity available. But you must admit the possibility that anything you post, even if anonymous, may be traced back to you. If you're posting something you wouldn't say in person in the same space, you probably shouldn't be posting it at all. (Call this the Golden Rule of the Internet!)

✦The internet is fast and reaches far.

Sure, we know in our heads the speed and reach of the internet. Those are some of the best qualities about it. Until . . . they're not. An accidental snap, an Insta comment left in anger, these things can be impossible to undo. Even if something can be taken down, a lot of people may have seen it first. (Or it could live on in a screenshot!)

✦Look out for predators.

The internet is home to a lot of creepy people. Unfortunately, you as an LGBTQ+ teen are more likely to become a target of some of these predators. But you can take precautions to make sure this doesn't happen to you, starting with keeping your private details private, and blocking/reporting someone at the first sign of trouble.

★ OKAY, WELL, NOW I'M TERRIFIED . . .

We didn't mean to go overboard there! But these are the realities of the internet that you—and all teenagers—need to be aware of as you're engaging online. Don't worry! We're here with some pro tips to help you navigate the tumultuous internet waters until you reach eighteen (and even then, these are really good rules).

* Always keep your full name and location confidential. This goes for social media sites, blogs, forums, etc.

* Only share pictures you want the world to see. And by "the world" we mean your mom. And your grandmother. Would you let them see those pictures? If not, reconsider hitting the share button.

* *Never* send nudes. To anyone. We're not saying this to be a buzzkill. But even on Snapchat or other auto-delete apps, information and pictures can still be stored. Having these pictures fall into the wrong hands can be devastating. Even if it's someone you trust, like your partner, just don't do it.

* Assume the worst (it's awful, we know!). There are people who will try to take advantage of you on the internet, both strangers and people you know. Be wise and wary. Be aware that some people create (convincingly) fake profiles.

* Be liberal with the block button. If anyone is creeping you out, harassing you, or just being a negative voice, cut 'em out! You won't miss them, we promise.

* Don't air dirty laundry on Facebook (or anywhere online). If the conflict that arises online is with people you know, address it in real life, if possible. Be mature. No one needs to read your drama on their newsfeed.

* Stay off dating apps till you're eighteen. Dating apps are fun and usually very safe. But to use them in high school you have to lie (they're for 18+), and

they are also places where predators take advantage of people—particularly young people, who just don't yet know what behavior is expected on dating apps.

★ Don't agree to meet people from the internet. However. If you are going to meet someone from the internet, follow these rules every time:

  ★ Always meet in a public place.

  ★ Always tell someone where you're going and when you will be home (and be home by then).

  ★ Arrange for your own transportation. Don't rely on a ride from a stranger.

★ Never share your passwords. With anyone. Sure, it seems cute now to have a joint Instagram account with your BFF. But you might not always feel that way. Make sure you're not giving personal and private info of any kind to your friends.

★ Be yourself! Don't get lost in the online reality. Don't live a double life.

★ HELP! I DIDN'T MEAN TO HIT SEND!

We've given you all this wonderful, sage advice. And now we're going to reveal a special secret: You're going to screw up! It's okay! We all do. The internet is just a seductive and tricky place, and we're all humans (with hormones).

No matter what online mess-up you've had, we promise your life isn't over. And there are probably some actions you can take.

If you've shared something you regret, seek help from trusted adults. Delete the post and apologize when appropriate. You may need to give it time, which does make healing and embarrassment easier.

If someone asks you for information, location, or personal property (including pics), don't share with them. Assess the situation (if you can, involve someone you trust), and report the person if necessary. If you already have shared something that puts you at risk, like your location, a photo, anything, tell a parent or trusted adult immediately. There are laws in place to protect you while you're under eighteen.

★ REMEMBER . . . INSTA ISN'T REAL LIFE

There's one last danger of social media and online use that we haven't talked about yet: comparison. Online comparison happens All. The. Time. If you think you're immune to it, well . . . you're not.

We all compare ourselves to others. And online, this can be especially dangerous. We see others' perfectly posed lives, flawless selfies, exciting adventures, and we feel like we're not enough. We feel less beautiful, less successful, less popular. We feel too queer, or not queer enough. Or queer in the wrong way. (Note: You cannot be queer wrong.)

Many mental health professionals are attributing rising rates of anxiety and depression in youth to increased social media use. Comparing our lives to the "reality" we see online can cause feelings of hopelessness and discouragement. When we're constantly measuring ourselves against others, we become more and more discontent with our lives. We stop seeing the beauty and joy around us.

The worst part about online comparison is that what makes us feel inadequate *isn't even real*. It's all created by someone to give the false appearance of perfection. Behind that computer is just a frumpy, lumpy, farting, burping human like the rest of us.

If you're scrolling online, endlessly comparing yourself and your life negatively with what you see on social media, just go ahead and delete that app. We're not saying that social media is the one and only cause of depression or anxiety (it's not). But having a little social media fast every now and then can do amazing things for your mind and spirit. You are perfect, queerfully and wonderfully made, and nothing you see on the internet can change that.

★ LAST THOUGHT

Basically, all this is just to say: Don't let the internet interfere with your totally bitchin' queer Christian life.

ISN'T A LITTLE ONLINE HARASSMENT JUST A PART OF BEING QUEER?

We asked this question earlier, regarding bullying, but the same question comes up online too. Because being on the internet, especially for young queer people, can be pretty difficult. If anything, it can be worse.

★ 42% of LGBTQ+ teens reported being bullied online (compared to 15% of their straight peers).

★ LGBTQ+ teens experienced nearly three times as much bullying online as their straight peers.

★ 27% of LGBTQ+ teens didn't feel safe online.

★ LGBTQ+ youth were four times more likely to be sexually harassed online.

★ 1 in 4 LGBTQ+ youth reported being bullied online specifically because of their sexual orientation or gender identity.

Online bullying is no small thing. Cyberbullying and harassment can affect your grades, your self-esteem, your mental health. Without action, it can be very dangerous.

But don't worry! Online harassment does *not* have to be a part of your life. There are many things you can do to protect yourself from online bullies.

★ BLOCK, BLOCK, BLOCK!

Many social media apps and online sites have ways to block people from interacting with you. Even your cell phone has a convenient "block number" option. If someone is harassing or bullying you, block them! Even if know them in real life—whether they're a former friend or just someone you are aware of—you should still block them. Blocking won't necessarily end cyberbullying, but you should try to limit a person's ability to make your life more difficult. Set boundaries that will help you feel safe. Blocking someone is not unkind. It's being smart and taking care of yourself.

★ REPORT

If you or someone you know is the victim of online harassment, you have a right to report this. And in some cases, you absolutely should. For example, sharing nude or sexual photos, with or without permission, is very often illegal. If the person pictured is under eighteen, it's child pornography and must be reported. No matter how embarrassed someone feels, it has to be taken care of by the law.

Whether harassment is sexual or not, though, you can still report what's happening to parents, school officials, or church leaders. If this is an internet troll making your life miserable, report the user to the site they're using. Facebook, YouTube, Twitter, and other sites are cracking down on online harassment and will often remove all negative content, or even block an online bully from using their site altogether. And again, after you report, block the offender. Get them out of your life.

Be on the lookout for anything that encourages self-harm or suicide. This kind of online behavior is serious and potentially illegal. Anyone pushing you or others toward harmful action can and should be reported to police. Even if you don't feel put in danger, it's likely they're doing the same to others, so it's important for this to be stopped.

★ KEEP THE EVIDENCE

When you're reporting online bullying, especially to law enforcement or other authorities, come with the evidence. Screenshots of any and all harassing messages via text or social media, email chains, photos sent without permission—whatever you've got, bring it. It may feel way too vulnerable to share this information with authorities, especially if you're not out yet. But at this point, you have a choice: allow the person to continue their harassment of you—and probably others—or put a stop to it.

Remember, you don't have to go to the authorities alone. Take a parent, a trusted and affirming adult, or a friend with you. You don't have to answer any questions that make you uncomfortable or that aren't related to the bullying you're reporting.

There are also some tools for anonymously reporting bullying and harassment. That depends on your city/state, so do some quick Googling to see if that's an option.

After you've reported the bullying, try not to dwell on, reread, or share these screenshots with lots of friends. Don't torture yourself. You've been brave, you've taken action, you've done what you can to put a stop to it. Now it's time to start moving on.

★ LAST THOUGHT

All of this probably makes the online world feel a little scary. But remember, when it comes to the internet, queer folks do it pretty much better than everyone. You, as a queer teen, are more likely to be using the internet for good things, like finding out health information, supporting your community, getting involved in civic activities, and making new friends. Instead of backing away from the internet because of bad actors, LGBTQ+ youth are diving in headfirst with the opposite message. You are making the internet a safer, more welcoming, and more accepting place just by being online.

Zoe, 24:

Like any stereotypical trans girl, I spend a lot of time in online communities. Both before and after my transition began, I interacted with close friends and complete strangers on the internet very frequently. How I did that, and what communities I chose to be a part of, changed drastically once I came out. I almost never talk to people I don't know outside of text chats, and even then, I am careful what I say about myself. It doesn't take much for someone to ask why I sound so "weird" in the middle of a video game or respond to me introducing myself with a stupid joke. If I am going to participate in a discussion where my status as a transgender woman will be apparent, I try not to be alone. Having someone there to back you up is key, because even if some of the strangers around you are on your side, they might not have the courage to stand up for you.

WHY DON'T I FIT IN WITH THE QUEER WORLD I SEE IN POP CULTURE?

It's easy to feel like you have to look, talk, or act a certain way to be queer in the right way. You have to love partying, attend Pride parades, excel in the world of fashion, be artsy, or love musical theater. These are clichés, of course. But they're clichés for a reason: our culture has a narrow and stereotypical view of what it means to be LGBTQ+.

If any of the above describe you, by the way, that's great. All of these things are wonderful. But it's very possible (if not quite probable) that not all of them—maybe none of them— describe you.

Well, guess what? Popular culture doesn't have the best grip on what it means to be queer. Because "what it means to be queer" is not a thing that can be captured with a one-size-fits-all list of characteristics, likes, and dislikes.

★ IN REAL LIFE

If you're constantly comparing yourself to the queer folks on TV, pause for a moment (no, seriously, pause whatever you're streaming right now). Here's the truth: pop culture rarely reflects reality. They might have some part of it right, but at the

end of the day, TV shows, movies, celebrities, and social media icons don't represent real life.

The LGBTQ+ community that you see in pop culture, while certainly queer and beautiful, is not the *only* expression of queerness. There are some spaces where young queer kids end up coming together, and often that becomes the "gay space" in a school or community. But LGBTQ+ people are just that—*people!* We are teachers and truck drivers, pastors and politicians, athletes and artists, baristas and boxers. The list is endless because being queer comes with endless possibility.

★ LOOK AT THE RAINBOW

The very symbol of our community, a rainbow, should remind you just how different and welcome everyone is in the LGBTQ+ community. Being your truest and most authentic self is part of the joy of being queer!

Constantly comparing yourself to others is easy. But it only pushes you further away from the community we all so desperately need. Every TV show or movie makes every character into, well, a *character*. And the truth is, most TV shows and movies are made by straight, cisgender people. Often, they're just writing us into their stories to serve the purpose they need.

Still. Not seeing yourself in pop culture—*representation*, this is called—can lead to isolation and depression. It's common to feel not queer enough, or not queer in the right way. So let us tell you: you are exactly the right amount queer, and in the most beautiful way.

The community called LGBTQ+ is just as wide and expansive and diverse as any other portion of humanity. Your queerness need not define you, nor should it ever be used to exclude you. Especially among other queers!

Your uniqueness adds so much value and depth to our community, and what you bring expands and deepens how others understand queer people. Welcome! We're so glad you're here.

Sophie, 19:
When I looked around at my LGBTQ+ friends, I saw a lot of diversity in interests and personality. Some of us were shy, some loud, some easygoing, some confrontational. Some were interested in sports, some in religion, writing, music. I was just as unique as any other teenager, but often when people saw that label of LGBTQ+, it became the most important thing to them and overshadowed everything else about me in their eyes. That was their fault, not mine.

WHY ARE BI AND PAN PEOPLE TREATED WORSE (EVEN BY OTHER QUEER FOLKS)?

Bisexuality and pansexuality are not exactly the same, but they have one crucial element in common: they both include attraction to multiple sexes and genders. And that means they also share one unfortunate consequence: they experience erasure.

erasure: noun

> the act of removing or destroying something.

For our purposes in discussing bi and pan erasure, we'll use GLAAD's language. They define bi-erasure as "a pervasive problem in which the existence or legitimacy of bisexuality (or pansexuality) is questioned or denied outright."

There are a few basic lines of erasure that tend to target bi and pan people. One comes from fellow queer people (halfway to gay), and the other can come from anyone (greedy sex-crazed maniacs!).

★ THE TRUTH ABOUT BI- AND PANSEXUALS

Bisexual and pansexual people are, by far, the largest group within the LGBTQ+ initialism. In fact, half (*half!*) of LGBTQ+ people identify as bisexual.

First of all, no matter what you're hearing about your identity, being bisexual or pansexual is not "halfway gay." It's true that *some* people who come out as bi do later come out gay or lesbian. It's also true that some people who come out as gay or lesbian later come out as bi. But most of the people who come out as bisexual or pansexual are . . . bisexual or pansexual.

Whatever garbage you hear about bi and pan people, it's just that. Garbage. Your love doesn't have to be limited, especially by the naysayers.

★ THE CONSEQUENCES OF BI-ERASURE

Many of the queer people you encounter will very likely have no problem with your bisexual or pansexual identity. We don't want to pit the queer community against each other here. But bi-erasure is common enough that it creates increased risks.

Because of bi-erasure and other pressures, bisexual youth tend to have higher rates of depression, family rejection, and social isolation than gay and lesbian folks. Bisexual people also hear more negative comments from family, leading to family isolation and rejection, which compounds all of the above-mentioned risks.

Bisexual and pansexual youth and adults are also generally less well-educated about their identities.

What little education there is on LGBTQ+ health focuses on lesbian and gay orientations. As a result, bisexual folks have higher rates of health disorders like STIs, heart disease, and cancer risks.

★ FIND YOUR PEOPLE!

If you've experienced bi-erasure, you are not alone, bi and pan friends! There are many real-life bi and pan people speaking up for and raising awareness about their community. And there are many bisexual and pansexual advocates among the broader LGBTQ+ community.

Bi representation is exploding, and that representation is helping! Gaby Dunn, Vivek Shraya, Sara Ramírez, and many others are out and proud bisexuals. Google the list of famous bisexuals and you'll be shocked at how many there are.

And while pansexuality doesn't have quite as many celebrities (remember, half of the queer community identifies as bi), there are people making those waves too: people like Janelle Monáe, Miley Cyrus, and Brendon Urie.

Read their stories, learn from their experiences, and add your own story to the list of legendary bisexual and pansexual queeros.

★ ONE LAST THING

Bisexuality doesn't mean that your attraction for people of different genders has to be the same. You may be romantically attracted to one gender and sexually attracted to another. Or attracted to boys for a few years, then attracted to everyone, then only to girls. Things may change over time. And that's all right.

And yes, one day you may identity as lesbian, gay, or something different. That doesn't mean your previous identity wasn't real. We're all on a journey of discovering our identities.

And yours is a beautiful process!

★ LAST (FOR REAL THIS TIME) THOUGHT

Just like with any other queer identity, you can and should be proud of your bisexuality or pansexuality. Know who you are and how to tell others confidently. Be an advocate for your community, but most importantly, be yourself! You don't owe anyone an explanation. You don't have to change everyone's mind. Just be proud and assured of who you are, no matter what others say.

★ A WORD FROM OUR BI/PAN FRIENDS . . .

Izzi, 26:

My previous partner (a cis-het man) was really unsettled by my sexuality, so I didn't discuss it much around him, which did make me feel isolated. And my church was your standard Midwest conservative congregation, so I was fairly closeted there as well. I don't feel that I've experienced isolation from the LGBTQ+ community. The online communities I'm a part of are extremely inclusive and all the people I've interacted with in person are accepting and encouraging people.

Hope, 21:

Biphobia / panphobia is still very real and alive today. As a pansexual woman, my identity and experiences have been denied many times from both the "straight" and the larger queer community because of those who are not convinced that it is a legitimate sexual orientation. Some think we're just "going through an experimental phase" and will eventually make up our minds. Some are even convinced that most of us will "take the easy way out" at the end of the day by succumbing to heteronormativity. These are all very inaccurate and harmful depictions of the bi/pansexual community, and lead many of us to remain in the closet because of a lack of support. I've received these comments even from some of my closest friends. However, the queer community is learning and growing every day alongside queer studies. Bi/Pansexual Visibility Days have been established to raise awareness about the bi/pansexual community. How I've responded has usually been:

"I understand that you are trying to make sense of my identity and my experiences. However, I think it's important to understand bi/pansexuality from the perspectives of those who identify as such and learn from questions instead of assumptions. I did not choose to be pansexual, and I also cannot cherry-pick convenient paths for myself because it doesn't work like that. Bi/pansexual visibility is important to me because the opposite of it is hate. Just like our other queer peers, we also yearn to be heard and supported. Take time to listen and love."

INTERLUDE:

An 8-Step Program for Queering Your Community

A quick and dirty guide to LGBTQ+ advocacy, for those ready to take it on:

1) **FIND YOUR PASSION.**

   Working to advance queer rights is a massively broad goal, and getting involved in something so broad will probably lead to burnout. Think about what motivates you. Is it access to gender-affirming spaces for trans and nonbinary people? Is it your church's lack of a clear policy on LGBTQ+ affirmation? Getting a GSA in your school? Finding an effort that specifically moves you will help keep you motivated throughout your work.

2) **KNOW YOUR ROLE.**

   What is it that *you* want to do? Are you comfortable out front in a protest? Or are you a planner? Fundraiser? Writer? Everyone has a role in advocacy, and nothing gets done without every role being filled. Find yours.

3) DO YOUR RESEARCH.
What, specifically, are the issues your community faces? What are the laws and policies in place? What has been tried?

4) FIND YOUR FELLOW ACTIVISTS.
It's very possible someone is already working on whatever issue motivates you to action. If they are, collaborate with them. If not, then recruit friends, classmates, anyone to join in your work. When it comes to making change, there is power in numbers.

5) MEET REGULARLY.
Once you and your like-minded queer advocates have gotten in touch, communicate on a regular schedule. Whether in person or online, the best way to keep people involved is to keep them talking to each other.

6) SET CLEAR GOALS.
This is connected to #1. But you are more likely to achieve your goals if your goals are specific and realistic. This doesn't mean you need to limit your ambitions. But it does mean you can achieve things that will help actual queer people in your community.

7) NEVER LOSE HOPE.
When it comes to LGBTQ+ rights, it can often feel like every step forward is followed by another step back. It can feel like your school, church, family, or community is just *never* going to change, no matter what you do. But change is possible. In fact, it's happening! Over just the past decade, huge strides have been made in terms of the number of people who are queer-affirming and the policies in place to provide equal rights to the queer community. Progress can seem excruciatingly slow, but we're moving forward—together.

8) LIVE YOUR TRUTH.
Advocating on behalf of the queer community means demonstrating the inherent, beautiful, God-given value of queerness. Being yourself feels good, and it makes it easier for others to live their truth too.

WHAT ABOUT PARTYING? (QUEER FOLK LIKE TO PARTY . . . I THINK?)

You're out, you're queer, it's time to party! Right?

Not everyone is into parties, queer or not. If you're not, then cool. No worries, move along. But if you are, then hey, good news: partying is a fantastic part of being queer. For many people, partying is just a pretty fun part of being a teenager.

Despite what all the terrified parents might think, there's nothing inherently wrong with partying. Having a good time with friends doesn't have to mean risky, bad-choice-filled, regret-worthy nights. So as we talk

about partying, remember that partying can and should be safe and carefree and FUN.

We just want to go over a few things to keep in mind while you're living it up with your friends. We aren't going to tell you what *not* to do. But we do want you to be informed and aware so you can make decisions that are right for you. The problem isn't partying. The problem is not knowing how to party smart. So, let's talk about how to do that!

★ DRUGS AND ALCOHOL

Sooo . . . turns out LGBTQ+ teens, in general, party harder than their straight and cisgender peers. And we mean that in the not-so-great way.

- ★ LGBTQ+ teens drink more and start earlier than their straight peers:
  - ★ 72% of LGBTQ+ students have used alcohol, compared to 60% of straight students.
  - ★ 21% of LGBTQ+ students had their first drink before the age of 13, compared to 14% of straight students.
  - ★ Binge drinking among lesbian and bisexual women is almost twice as high as among their straight peers.
- ★ LGBTQ+ teens are using drugs at higher rates than their straight peers:
  - ★ 50% of LGBTQ+ students have smoked marijuana, compared to 35% of straight students.
  - ★ Recreational use of prescription drugs: 24% of LGBTQ+ students; 13% of straight students.
  - ★ Cocaine use: 8% of LGBTQ+ students; 4% of straight students.

Remember, these are just numbers. They're not you! We are not trash-talking queer young people here. There are a *lot* of reasons our community is using alcohol and drugs more than cis-het teens—mainly because queer teens face a lot more discrimination, family rejection, and social pressures, leading to increased rates of anxiety and depression. It is not *because some of us love to party*. The fact remains, though, that you're more likely to be using drugs and alcohol. Or you're at least more likely to encounter friends who are.

It's no fun to hear this, but teenagers really don't know what they're doing with drugs and alcohol. So, let's talk some guidelines for how to party safe.

★ FIRST UP: DRINKING

You shouldn't drink. It's illegal and dangerous for teenagers to consume alcohol. If you're caught, you could get in serious trouble—whether that trouble comes from home, school, or the police. If the police don't deter you, remember that legal and academic records, even pictures on social media, will affect college admissions if you apply, and job applications.

And we have to mention: combining alcohol and sexual activity in your teenage years (or anytime, really) doesn't end well. From blurring the lines of consent to blackout assaults, sex can go wrong very quickly when one or both partners are drunk. So seriously, just don't do it.

And yet, we are not ignorant. We know the reality. We know that you're a teenager, in a social world of some kind or other. The government reports that by age eighteen, 60 percent of Americans have consumed alcohol. So, when it comes to drinking (which you shouldn't do!), always remember:

- ★ Never take a drink from a stranger.
- ★ Never take your eyes off your drink. If you do, or if someone hands it back to you, get a new one.

- *Slow doowwwn* (honestly, teens often don't know their tolerance or how quickly booze can hit). Don't do shots or drinking games. It's terrible for your body, and the hangovers are atrocious.

- Always travel in groups and don't get separated. Don't go to a party where you don't know anyone.

- Never get in a car with anyone who's been drinking. And, obviously, DO NOT drive after drinking. Call a cab or your parents. You think they'll be mad about you drinking? Well, how will they like you getting a DUI, or worse?

★ WHAT ABOUT DRUGS?

Just don't do them.

Look. We get it. We said don't drink, and then we gave some guidelines for drinking because there's an understanding that many of you are probably going to drink at least once in high school or, at the very least, be in the proximity of drinking.

But we are not doing that with drugs. Drugs are not a good idea. They're harmful, are easily tampered with, and can affect your whole life in ways you may not realize, including getting kicked out of school, cut from your sport, fired from a job, and arrested. Not only that, but drugs harm your body, emotions, and mind.

★ WHAT IF I DON'T LIKE TO PARTY?

Not the partying type? No worries! That doesn't mean you are any less queer, or any less fun or exciting. In fact, it doesn't mean anything, other than parties just aren't your thing. That's true of lots of folks (and lots of queer folks).

Just skip the parades (so many of us do!), skip the dance parties, and . . . do whatever you love to do instead. Which is just super great! There's no shame in not partying. And there's no shame in partying either.

★ ASK YOURSELF THE "WHY" QUESTION

Whether you're a partier or not, whether you would never drink or like to drink, we want to pose a couple questions. And we want you to answer. No, seriously, grab a piece of paper and jot down these questions and your thoughts.

- ✦ Why do you think smoking/drinking/drugs is more common among LGBTQ+ people?

- ✦ If you want to drink/smoke/do drugs, why? Is it peer pressure? To have fun and build your community? Is it to dull your sadness? Give you courage?

There are no right or wrong answers here. But whatever you say about these questions makes a huge difference. Think about what you write. How do you feel about the reasons you gave?

★ LAST THOUGHT

Remember, there's nothing inherently wrong with partying. It can bring fun, community, and great memories! But if you can't party safe (or just don't want to party), then don't party at all! Whatever you choose to do, be smart. Be wise. And remember that the choices you make now will impact your future.

OKAY, BUT I'M SERIOUS. HELP! I'M, LIKE, REALLY HORNY!

Are you thinking about sex again? *Again?!* Understandable. You're a teenager. And if you're someone who wants sex, your teenage hormones tend to bring these thoughts and desires to the front of your mind over and over (and over and over) again. And that's okay. Totally normal. Maybe it's even kind of fun?

Remember that sex and thoughts about sex aren't wrong. It's how your thoughts and desires turn into action that matters. Are you practicing safe sex? Are you honoring your partner and their body? Are you aware that sex isn't all about you? If you're not, no matter how much you think about sex, that's where you need to keep it: in your head.

Even if you are just thinking about "it," though, there's nothing to be ashamed of! It's okay to talk about sex with a trusted friend, a therapist, or even your parents (gasp!). It can be extremely helpful to process where you're at on the subject.

We have a few more sex-related questions coming, and feel free to refer back to our first question on this too. But we're just scratching the surface of what is a lifelong relationship between you, your body, and your partners' bodies.

I'M NEVER HORNY. SHOULD I BE CONCERNED?

Popular culture sexualizes everything. No one is safe from over-sexualization. And yet. Even in the hyper-sexualized popular imagination, queer people somehow remain the most randy-and-ready of all the sex-crazed maniacs. Some voices out there would have you believing that the entirety of our identity is wrapped up in sex.

But we want you to know something: that's ridiculous.

You—and your queerness—are not defined by the sex you are or are not having. You can be confident in who you are regardless of whether you have or haven't had sex. Don't let someone question your identity based on sex.

So when people ask, "How do you know you're queer if you haven't dated/had sex/etc.?" all you have to say is, "Because I know who I am." No one else needs to know or understand for that to be true.

★ SELF-REFLECTION TIME

There's no one reason why someone doesn't want to have sex. But it's important to think about why you're not interested.

Don't force yourself to do anything or even think anything that doesn't feel right for you.

Instead, do some self-examination. Learn more about yourself. Put into words where you're at and why. Not only is it helpful for understanding yourself, but it can also help you organize your thoughts, making it easier to process where you're at with others.

Here are some questions you can ask yourself about having (or not having) sex:

* Am I afraid? If so, what specifically is creating that fear?

* Am I self-consciousness about my knowledge/body?

* Am I simply not having sexual thoughts? (This is totally normal.)

* Does thinking about sex give me shame?

* What have my parents, church, and community taught me about sex? Do I agree with that teaching?

Read over your answers. How do you feel?

Whatever your decision on sex, be thoughtful and safe and patient.

★ ASEXUALITY

Some people who are never horny are, by definition, not sexually attracted to others. This is called *asexuality*, and it's a valid, real sexual orientation within the queer community.

Asexuality means that someone lacks sexual attraction. That's it. You can be interested in dating, romance, marriage, everything involved in social relationships. You can be a lesbian, gay, or bi asexual, meaning you have same-gender romantic attraction without the sexual attraction. Basically, asexuals don't have hormonal, chemical, or physical interest in sex, and if that sounds like you, then read more on asexuality. It might be you forever, or for now, or never. Queerness is a process, and nothing has to be set in stone.

★ CELIBACY

You won't hear much about celibacy (fully abstaining from sex or marriage) in the queer community unless you're in the kind of church, well, that promotes things like celibacy for queer people. But it's worth pointing out that asexuality has nothing to do with celibacy. Some Christian communities teach that anyone who is queer is required to be celibate now and forever. That is a teaching based on their belief that being queer is a sin. It isn't, as you hopefully know by now. (If not, then go back to page 31!)

Some churches—including some queer-affirming churches—encourage celibacy for both queer and non-queer people who are not in a long-term, committed, monogamous relationship. If you agree with that teaching, that is perfectly legit as well. These matters are up to you.

Just know that not having sex is not the same as not wanting to have sex. If you want to be celibate, go ahead and good luck. But celibacy is not a sexual orientation.

★ LAST THOUGHT

It's okay if you don't want to have sex. Ignore all the voices saying otherwise, and listen to yourself. Never give in to pressure to have sex when you're not ready. Have sex when you're ready and want to. And if you don't want to, then don't.

CAN I LOOK AT PORN?

Do you mind if we have a quick discussion about porn? Teens love talking about porn, right?

No? Oh, you think talking about porn is awkward and uncomfortable? You'd rather literally do anything other than talk about porn? Well, that's why it's *so* important for us to do it here. Because people *don't* have a lot of healthy discussion about pornography, it can be hard for anyone to figure out what to think about it.

Okay, let's get into porn.

⭐ WHAT IS PORN?

Pornography is, in most Christian communities, a dirty word. But what porn actually is, well, that's harder to define. Broadly, pornography is simply any kind of media intended to sexually arouse or excite someone. Pornography is as old as humans (it's been around literally forever), and it can come in a lot of different forms—from erotic magazines to sexually explicit novels or photographs. And of course, it's everywhere on the internet.

★ WHO LOOKS AT PORN?

A lot of people! Probably more than you think. It's really hard to find accurate data on how many people watch porn (wonder why that is? *cough SHAME cough*), but estimates tend to align right around here:

> **Two-thirds of teenage and young adult boys seek out porn at least once a month and one-third of teenage and young adult girls seek out porn at least once a month. (This poll used outdated gender binary language.)**

So, yes. Lots and lots of people watch or view porn. The more important question is, Why?

Some people use porn as a way of exploring their own sexuality. Others view porn with their romantic partners. They view porn as a way to explore sexuality safely and without harming someone else (which may or may not be accurate, depending on the kind of porn you're endorsing). And others—well, to be blunt, they just want to get off.

Now, we say a lot of people look at porn, but it's also true that a lot of people *don't* view porn. Again, for many reasons: moral issues; concerns about the safety and well-being of the participants; pornography's negative effect on how people view sex and sex partners, particularly women, given the enormous number of men who watch it. Others just may not find pornography arousing.

★ WHY SHOULD (OR SHOULDN'T) I LOOK AT PORN?

Let's talk about some potential benefits of using porn. Yes, there are real benefits to porn for mature queer teenagers (no matter what your pastors or parents might say).

For starters, porn can be a safe way to explore your sexuality. You can learn about your body and pleasure and how to make the most of both. You can also take that information, when applicable, and put it to use on your partner's body.

There is also the education (it's misguided education, but still) that can come from watching queer porn. This is because queer sex education is largely absent from America's schools. There are not a lot of places to learn the *hows* of queer sex. Queer porn is one of those places. By *queer porn*, we mean porn made specifically for queer audiences. That is very different than freely available porn with same-gender participants made explicitly for straight people (more on that below).

Finally, you can watch porn with your partner, which can open up new conversations about sex and pleasure, stimulate our natural arousal systems, or it can just be a silly fun thing to experience together.

So, if those are the benefits, what are the costs? Truth is, there are A LOT more costs than benefits when it comes to pornography. Here are a few of the top problems with the majority of porn:

1. PORN ISN'T REAL.

Literally. Porn is a fantasy performed by actors. Treating porn like it's real often creates unhealthy and inaccurate expectations of sex. For example, pornography usually features stereotypically "beautiful" people performing exaggerated, even dangerous sexual acts. Everyone's *always* in the mood for sex in pornography. And that sex is always "perfect." No awkward moments or average experience.

2. PORN CAN PERPETUATE HARMFUL COMPARISONS.

Porn is never intended for real-world comparisons. Not the way the actors look and not the behaviors the actors engage in. These comparisons can make you feel bad about how you look, and it can make you feel bad about what you do, or don't do, with your partner. Comparing yourself to porn is a pathway to sexual disappointment. And sex is great!

3. PORN CAN BE ADDICTING.

Watching pornography releases chemicals in your brain that activate your pleasure center. And that feeling might bring you back to porn more than you'd like, even to a point where it's difficult to get aroused without it. This obviously isn't a great place to be. Your future partner is going to benefit from you having a healthy relationship with porn, *not* from you being addicted to it. Pornography can also be isolating. Users can become disinterested in real-life sexual relationships.

4. PORN IGNORES CONSENT.

By its very nature, porn assumes consent. Simply by watching, you are consenting to anything that appears before you. Are you comfortable with that? And are you comfortable making that assumption for all those involved in what you're watching? Remember: porn is not real. Consent is real, and it can never, *ever* be assumed.

5. NOT ALL PORN IS CREATED EQUAL.

There is a lot of very, very bad porn online. And as free online porn gets more and more popular, things behind the camera get worse. Some pornography results from sex trafficking and slavery. Some is created without basic health and safety requirements being met, leading to spreading of STIs and other negative health outcomes. And some porn is violent and inherently degrading.

The only way to be *sure* about what you are consuming is to pay for it. If you won't pay for it, *at least do your research.* Most LGBTQ+ websites have articles pointing you to safely made pornography for queer audiences.

As a whole, the online pornography industry is very problematic (that's an understatement). It's filled with misogyny, abuse, and exploitation. A lot of pornography is harmful to women in particular, portraying them as only sexual beings to be dominated. Yes, there is healthy queer porn and a healthy way to consume it. But many people don't put in that effort. And if you aren't going to do that base level of work, then just leave porn alone.

★ ALTERNATIVES TO PORN

There are a lot of ways to learn about and explore queer sex without porn. For example, use your imagination! Seriously. No porn will ever be as satisfying or specifically tailored to your own sexual pleasure as what you imagine for yourself. Being able to "get there" without the use of pornography is more pleasurable too.

If you really want external stimulation, there are still plenty of healthy, safe alternatives to porn. Like, draw a fantasy picture or write your own sexy story. This may sound really, really corny, but we promise you that it works, and again, it works *better* than pornography. And you can share it with your partner, and they will think it works A LOT BETTER THAN PORN!

★ SO WHAT SHOULD I DO?

If you are going to watch porn, then you should be honest with yourself about what you're watching, where it comes from, and what risks it poses. Don't kid yourself. Know your boundaries, and remember, porn is a fantasy.

If you're not going to watch porn—cool. Good for you. That is a healthy and smart choice! Remember to be respectful of other people's choices and preferences, and approach porn in an ethical way.

HOW DO I KNOW WHEN I'M READY FOR . . . IT? (WE MEAN SEX)

There's a difference between thinking about sex, wanting to have sex, and then actually . . . well . . . doing . . . *it*.

Just because you're thinking about sex doesn't mean you're ready. Just because you *want* sex doesn't mean you're ready. Just because your friends are doing it doesn't mean you should, either. So how do you know when you're ready? Well, we can't say for sure.

There's no handbook for this. No specific age restrictions or test you have to pass. It's not like getting your driver's license. A lot of queer youth have sex in high school (48 percent, compared to 39 percent of straight people). Some wait until graduation or college or even marriage. Some view sex causally; others want it only in serious relationships.

Everyone has a different answer to this question because we all have different views of sex and relationships. There's no one right or wrong answer here. You just have to figure out who you are, what your values are when it comes to sex, and if you feel prepared enough to consider it. Those are big questions.

★ WHAT DO I THINK ABOUT SEX?

When deciding if you're ready for sex or not, a good first question is, How do you *actually* feel about sex? Does the thought make you nervous (or scared out of your mind)? Maybe you feel excited (giddy as a child on Christmas)? Maybe both? Maybe neither? How do you view sex in your relationship? Do you think your partner is thinking as seriously about your relationship or sex as you are? Do you want sex to be casual or a serious step? Is your partner pressuring you or threatening to break up if you don't?

Being able to honestly answer these questions will tell you a lot about whether you should move forward.

When you're ready to move on, it's time to get specific:

- ★ Do you know, specifically, what kind of sex you're preparing to have? What does it look like in your head?

- ★ How do you expect to feel after having sex?

- ★ Are you prepared for a negative emotional response (shame, self-loathing, regret)?

- ★ What are your boundaries—emotionally and physically—and can you hold to them even in the heat of the moment?

- ★ Is this sex solely physical, or is it emotional? Know your expectations and be ready for either.

- ★ How well do you know your partner? Will they be discreet about what happens? (Please don't hook up on your first time, and pretty please don't hook up with someone outside of your age range.)

- ★ What will you say when your parents find out? (Spoiler: They probably will. Have a plan.)

Whew! That was a lot of questions!

Knowing when you're ready can take time. In fact, it *should* take time. Sex is a beautiful part of your life, and it deserves thoughtful consideration. Trust us, it will still be amazing even if you go for it prepared. So, grab your journal and try answering some of the above questions. Or spend some time just objectively thinking about sex. Okay, not like fantasy stuff here (do that too—just not *right now*). What do you *actually* think about sex?

★ WHY NOW? OR NOT NOW?

You've probably got a lot of voices telling you when you should or shouldn't have sex (and most of them are probably saying, "DON'T, FOR THE LOVE OF GOD, PLEASE DON'T!!!" or something close to that). That's because people—especially heterosexual, cisgender parents—often project their own values around sex onto younger people.

But this is *your* decision. You should never feel pressured one way or another when it comes to sex. Your parents and pastors do not have control over your body. It doesn't matter what your friends are doing. It doesn't matter what anyone—queer or not—has to say.

That includes your partner.

Don't move quickly toward sex just to please a partner. Your partner should always, *always, ALWAYS* respect your decisions and readiness (or not) for sex. EVERY TIME. If they do not, you may need to consider whether this is a healthy relationship for you. We know that's hard to hear. But your safety, both physically and emotionally, is way more important than another person's desires. Remember, this is your choice.

★ SAFETY FIRST

If you feel like you're ready for sex, that's great! Why did you come to this decision? Have you talked about it with others?

Who and why? Have you taken protective measures? We talked about this earlier, but it's worth repeating. Make sure you're practicing safe, protected sex. That means condoms, lube (not Vaseline or some other substitute), and other necessary measures based on the kind of sex you are having.

★ SO . . . YOU'RE READY!

If you're going to have sex, have fun! But . . . we have one last question: Do you have what you need to keep yourself safe? Let's make this as unsexy as possible.

Have realistic expectations. You might have an orgasm; you might not. It might be "good sex," but it probably will look more like first sex: messy, confusing, scary, funny, or over before it begins. All of that is part of the process, and you and your partner should lean into the "first time" nature of the experience together.

Amid all of that, though, remember: It shouldn't be painful in the way that makes you want to stop. If it is, STOP. Actually, if you want to stop for *any* reason, stop. Because there's always next time, and sex is something worth getting right.

Talk to your partner about the experience before, during, and after. But in addition, plan to have someone to debrief the experience with later. Talk honestly about how you feel and what you learned. Make sure this person is someone trusting and affirming, who loves you.

★ SO . . . YOU'RE NOT READY . . .

If you're not ready to have sex yet, that's awesome. No, really, it is. Pop culture likes to make us think that everyone is having sex soon, and All. The. Time. But, spoiler alert, that's not actually true!

Plenty of people wait to have sex until their late teens or twenties, or until marriage. There is no shame in waiting to have sex. Like, seriously. At all. If you're uncertain about sex, then wait a while longer. It's okay to turn down an opportunity for sex, and anyone who says otherwise is not a partner you want to be with.

★ ONE LAST THING

We do not think you should have sex before you are out of high school. You have a full lifetime to explore your queer identity and all the fabulous sex that will bring. There is, honestly, no reason to rush this. But we know a lot of you will (some of us did, too). And the most important thing we can say about it is: Take care of yourself and your partner. If you do that, all will be well.

HOW DO QUEER PEOPLE EVEN HAVE SEX?

When we hear the word *sex*, we usually think of, well . . . straight, heteronormative sexual intercourse. In this normie version of sex, there's a woman and a man, foreplay, penetration, orgasm, the end. This popular conception of "sex" comes from a very dumb thing our culture does: we glamorize sex while *never actually talking about sex*. It's a massively oversimplified idea of sex—even for straight sex—and it has nothing to do with queer sex. That's because of an even dumber thing our culture does: totally ignore queer sex.

Which means your questions probably don't get a lot of attention in the sex ed classes you've been in. Sex education for LGBTQ+ teens is not great. No. It's terrible. Even today, in schools and churches, queer sex ed is terrible! Many queer teens often feel abandoned when it comes to this topic because they don't want their sex life to be like normie straight sex. You want the good, fun, all-out queer sex!

We're not going to go into graphic detail here. But we do want to make sure you know how to have fun, safe, healthy sex *whenever* you decide you're ready.

★ THE FREEDOM OF QUEER SEX

Don't tell your straight friends, but you're going to have much better sex than they are. The beautiful thing about queer sex—like queer relationships, and queer life in general—is that there are no norms or assumptions or preexisting roles to play. We challenge and reject stereotypes and expectations just by doing . . . anything.

So, when a "man" has sex with a "woman," there's a certain expectation that their sex will look pretty close to what culture has taught them it should look like. But when two women, or two men, or a trans woman and a nonbinary person or a trans man and a gay man get in bed together, there just is no preexisting assumption about what the heck is going to happen. You have to figure it out for yourselves, and that is so, so freeing.

And that doesn't just happen the first time you have sex. You get to re-figure it out with every new partner, because prior assumptions don't carry over. Exploring queer sex is an exciting and ever-changing experience. Go into it with the appropriate, adventurous spirit.

★ THOUGHTS ON SAFETY

If it's not obvious, let's make this clear: When we say be adventurous, we don't mean take unnecessary risks. And just like straight sex, you need to be protected and safe.

Safety means protection: Any exchange of bodily fluids poses a risk of sexually transmitted infections or diseases. So be prepared.

Safety means physical comfort and pleasure: use lube.

And once more for the balcony: Safety means consent. You need to get it and you need to give it, in all of your sexual experiences.

★ LAST THOUGHT

So how do queer people have sex? All the ways! You're on a journey of discovering your needs, your desires, your sexuality. It's okay for this to be a process. It's okay to try new things. As you do, be smart and be safe.

CAN I GO TO THE LOCAL QUEER SEX SHOP? (AND WHY WOULD I?)

This might seem like a strange question. What could be more embarrassing than being seen entering a sex shop?!

Well, first of all, we're not talking about magazine and porno shops with big XXX signs over the doorway. Depending on where you live, such places might be the only sex-based store for hundreds of miles. We get that, but we are talking about another kind of sex shop.

★ WHAT'S AT A QUEER SEX SHOP?

We are talking about sex-positive, queer, and queer-friendly stores.

Yes, they have sex toys. But they often offer a lot more too, and very often, sex shops are the most well-resourced, educated places to ask questions as a newly out queer person.

They can provide classes, fashion, books, lubrication, and sexual intimacy merchandise, as well as opportunities for shame-free conversation. How many places can you ask a very, very specific question about your queerness to an adult who will, in all likelihood, be totally free of judgment? Whatever you have to ask, it's NOTHING compared to what some folks will be into.

All of this assumes that you are out, live in proximity to such a place, and are assertive enough to undertake this adventure. If you're not, you're not. But if you *are* such a person, we just want to give you options.

★ WHY GO TO A QUEER SEX SHOP?

There aren't many places where a queer person can go to shop for queer-specific merchandise in a judgment-free environment. We especially want to highlight how beneficial such a place can be for trans, genderqueer, and nonbinary teens. These are places you can often buy, and learn how to use, all kinds of queer garments, including gaffes, binders, and corsets. It is crucial to *learn how to use* these items! Many people buy them online, but sustained incorrect usage of binders or gaffes can be painful and dangerous.

You might still be thinking: *Yeah, that's all good, but what if somebody sees me!?!* And you're right, that's a risk. We just want you to know what your options are. And shops like these allow young queer people, maybe for the first time, to:

- ★ have a salesperson who is understanding, sensitive, and nonjudgmental.

- ★ shop outside the male/female binary.

- ★ have access to sex education and equipment explicitly made for queer people and bodies.

- ★ exist—if only for a few minutes—outside of the heteronormative world.

You may not have a need or desire to go to a queer sex shop. Now or ever. But keep in mind that queer sex shops are much more than the stigma would suggest. These places are sex-positive and non-secretive. They can offer great resources for the LGBTQ+ community.

DOES IT GET BETTER?

Things are improving for the our community. As LGBTQ+ advocacy continues and more queer people are speaking out, we're seeing acceptance increase for all queer identities. At the same time, more church communities are moving toward affirming theology and recognizing the harm involved in trying to change someone's sexual orientation or gender identity.

This is, to be clear, great news. But to any individual queer Christian young person, it is also completely unhelpful. If you're feeling scared, anxious, depressed, overwhelmed, or ashamed, who cares about a 5 percent increase in acceptance of queer rights?

What you care about, and what you *should* care about, is how to make things better for you.

★ WHAT DOES "GETTING BETTER" ACTUALLY MEAN TO ME?

This question is one for you to answer individually.

We don't know what "it" is, specifically, for you. Ask yourself, then: What's missing? How would you like your life to look different than it does today? These aren't rhetorical questions, either. Imagine your life as you would like to see it: Are you still at your church? Are you still at any church? Are you dating? Married? Living in a big city? Living in your hometown?

Okay, now ask yourself: What would it take to have that life?

You can achieve that life, but we're going to be real with you. You won't get it through magic and positive thinking. Building a fabulous queer life requires work (everything does, really).

The truth for many is that things may not get better until you're out of your parents' house. Or out of your current church. Or out of your high school. If you are in a position in which all of these—family, church, school—are already affirming, then great. It will *still* get better as you start your own independent life.

Whatever a fulfilling life looks like for you, focus on how you can achieve it in the future, and surround yourself with affirming and loving people who will encourage and help you along the way. Know that you're not alone in this.

★ IT'S A PROCESS

Life is a whole lot like queerness: it's a process. It's always changing and so are we. No matter what age you are, you're still going to be figuring things out. Learning who you are and what you want. Forgiving others and letting go. Healing through heartbreak and celebrating new opportunities. But yes, even this gets better.

It gets better, in part, because we get better at living. At knowing how to take care of ourselves and others. At asking for what we need, and making boundaries to protect ourselves from what we don't. The more you learn about yourself, the easier it is for you to make it better.

★ WHEN THINGS DON'T FEEL BETTER

"Getting better" means, in part, learning to recognize when things are not as they should be. Which means noticing a spike in your anxiety or depression, and responding accordingly. It means recognizing a risky behavior or situation, and learning how to avoid it. Stuff is still going to happen. But when it does, see it for what it is. Acknowledge when you feel low. And when you need help, ask for it. Also, make note of those times when you feel great, and thank God for them.

★ FACING ALL THE FACTORS

We'll be honest. Some of you out there will have it harder than others. It's not fair, but life doesn't deal everyone the same hand. There are lots of factors that account for the unfairness of being a queer Christian: where you're born, what your parents believe, what kind of church you go to, which teachers or pastors you're randomly assigned.

Being queer does mean being a member of a minority community, and it can—but doesn't always—make things harder. It's possible you are among those who suffer intersectional discrimination, and that makes things even harder.

Our friends of color, our disabled friends, our low-income friends are facing other struggles in addition to LGBTQ+ discrimination. When facing intersectionality, it can be hard to see a way forward. But there is still So. Much. Hope. For you!

Who we are is out of our hands, just like our queer identity is out of our hands. Every part of us is created by God, inherently good and deserving of love. We have to accept that, and love ourselves and our queerness, whether or not those around us do too.

★ NEVER STOP BEING YOUR BEAUTIFUL QUEER SELF

There is a world waiting for you, a queer life that is full and beautiful and has room for every part of who you are: queer, Christian, completely beautiful. The opportunity to live your authentic life is coming. If you read this book, and still haven't come out to anyone, *great!* We love you. Please wait until you're ready.

If you are out and loud and proud, surrounded by family and friends and a faith community that fully supports your queerness, *great!* We love you, and are so happy for you.

If things are bad right now—for any reason—and you don't see how they can improve, we love you, and we're sorry.

With time, you will know yourself better. You will love yourself better. You will be better equipped; you will have a fuller, more accepting community. And you will get better at protecting yourself.

God loves you *and* your queerness. And so do we. And because we love you, we are going to say it one more time: It gets better (because you are queer, and queer is *best*).

Kaya, 25:

> It gets so much easier. I grew up in a church that would have hated me if they knew who I really was. The doctrines I was forced to internalize and repeat for years made me think that I could never go to church again. It wasn't until I walked into a church that had rainbow flags and was greeted by a young

gay woman who delivered the sermon that I realized that Christianity has a wide spectrum of acceptance. I was used to one end, where an old man drones from his chair about how we are all going to hell before an organ plays a sad song. When I realized that church could be young, accepting, and joyous, I found out that I could be Christian and still be me. Even better, being Christian could make me an even better version of myself. I have so many more opportunities to use my talents to make the world a better place because I found my church. I only hope that you are able to find a place in the world that makes you feel as loved and empowered as I did.

WE'VE REACHED THE END. GIVE ME THE REPRESENTATION I NEED AND TELL ME WHAT A QUEER FUTURE LOOKS LIKE.

This is the exciting part—the rest of your beautiful, queer life! And we promise, your life, your story, is going to be pretty amazing. Just take a look at the stories of those who've shared with us throughout this book. Your queer Christian life, like theirs, will be wonderful.

You're going to have so many adventures . . .

Missy, 21:

I see a lot in my future. In a few months I get out of uni and I'm moving to a different city. Where I'm planning to live has an LGBTQ+-affirming church in walking distance, and I'm insanely excited about attending there. I also want to get married, so I'm hoping to one day find another queer Christian woman who I'll fall in love with and she'll want to be my wife. I'm also going into the film industry, and I'm excited to tell more inclusive stories, not just about queer people but about queer Christian people. To let the world know we exist and to let those people working things out know that it's going to be okay.

You'll fall in love, maybe a few times . . .

Charlotte, 25:

Watching her watch the snow falling from the heavens, my heart skipped a beat . . . and then began to pump so fast it almost hurt. And at long last I identified the feeling in my chest, the feeling that had sprouted back in autumn and that had been growing, growing, only to blossom now: it was love. Not platonic, affectionate love—No: this was a kind of love I had never allowed to blossom inside of me. This was romantic love.

You'll chase your biggest ideas . . .

Xavi, 26:

I have a dream of getting my master's in applied linguistics and working in the mission field in Bible translation. Being gay isn't going to hold me back in the work I desire to do for the international church . . . I see a bright future ahead of me. And the complete assurance that I am eternally loved and accepted by a high and holy God.

You'll be an advocate . . .

Hannah, 21:

As a queer Christian, despite the dark times we have been through, I still have hope that in the future, our children will be able to love freely and proudly. I see myself being a persistent advocate for LGBTQ rights and respect in the church as well in my home country. I see myself being a friend and family to queer Christian youths and working together with others to always empower them in churches and countries.

And you'll meet so many other advocates too!

Kim, 21:

I see myself as an advocate for the intersectionality between spirituality and sexuality. I run a group focused on this topic at my university called Religious Rainbow and want to do more educating across my hometown that being gay does not make me a heathen and that my sexuality is a gift.

Mel, 19:

I see a bright future for my community and me. Personally, I see a future full of activism and change, but also a life of joy and peace. Whether or not we dedicate our lives to the work of affirmation and reconciliation, we have the power to love and support one another, to foster loving and healthy relationships, romantic and platonic, create found families, rejoice in solidarity and fellowship. We have both the right and the ability to love and be loved, and I wholeheartedly believe that is what God has in store for us.

You'll get frustrated . . .

Sarah, 25:

Sometimes it feels like standing at the bottom of a mountain and looking up. It can be hard to imagine a future sometimes when the Christian community still has a long way to go in affirming queer relationships. Ideally, I see a community in which I can be in a same-sex relationship and/or marriage and reap the same benefits that opposite-sex relationships have afforded to them. This includes being able to serve in the church by being a part of the music ministry, kids ministry, youth ministry, teach an adult Bible study, attend marriage or parenting conferences, receive advice or counseling from a pastor about the relationship if needed, attend events with my spouse or significant other, and anything and everything else.

And you'll see victory.

Cass, 27:

I am really energized to see more congregations supporting LGTBQIA+ folks in their congregation and outside of it. This for me is an example of God helping people to be more loving and compassionate in our world. I hope that we can show that Christianity is not a religion of hate and rejection even though that is how some people practice it. We can model Christ's love for the world.

You'll make mistakes—oh-so-many mistakes . . .

Kris, 23:

I'm not perfect. I still have a lot of bitterness towards the church and those that don't "agree" with my love. I still struggle within my friendships with those that condemn homosexuality and my worlds don't always collide well, but I'm trying to embrace all of me and let it show.

And you'll grow because of them.

Di, 25:

I am rewriting my future as you read this. I am finding friends who are affirming and inclusive. This also means finding a faith community that is affirming and inclusive as well. As a beginning and aspiring songwriter, I am changing my message to speak on the realities and injustices that I have experienced and to give/create a community of hope—where everyone is welcomed. I'm finally stepping out to be me and finding purpose in life and purpose for this pain that I have been through.

You'll always have questions . . .

Xi, 18:
I believe my future will be full of questioning, not only of myself, [like] who am I as a person, but also of other people's questions, since the church doesn't spread its message of love as much as its message of who fits in and who gets left out.

But you'll learn to love them.

Isaiah, 25:
To me, that is what a queer life is: a queer life constantly questions, breaks down, builds up, transcends. A queer life refuses to be cowed or shamed into silence; it does not keep its head down or eyes shut to injustice. If it turns the other cheek, it is never out of acquiescence to power but only ever to subvert and expose that power— to compel the oppressor to stop and think, or be shamed themselves.

You'll raise up a new generation—*your* generation.

Whatever you do, wherever you go, know that above all else, you are so wonderfully made by God. Your life has endless—and we mean *endless*—value. Your voice, your story, those are once-in-a-universe! *YOU* are a once-in-a-universe creation!

So go out there and live your life to the fullest. Go with the knowledge of who you are. Go with your questions and your passions. We can't wait to see how you change the world!

GLOSSARY

advocate: 1 *noun* : A person who actively works to end intolerance, educate others, and support social equity for a marginalized group. **2** *verb* : to actively support or plea in favor of a particular cause; the action of working to end intolerance or educate others.

homophobia: The fear and hatred of or discomfort with people who are attracted to members of the same sex.

agender: Having no (or very little) connection to the traditional system of gender, no personal alignment with the concepts of either man or woman, and/or seeing oneself as existing without gender. Sometimes called "gender neutrois," "gender neutral," or "genderless."

ally: A person who is not LGBTQ+ but shows support for LGBTQ+ people and promotes equality in a variety of ways.

androgynous: Identifying and/or presenting as neither distinguishably masculine nor distinguishably feminine.

aromantic: Experiencing little or no romantic attraction to others and/or having a lack of interest in romantic relationships/behavior. Aromanticism exists on a continuum from people who experience no romantic attraction or have no desire for romantic activities, to those who experience low levels, or romantic attraction only under specific conditions. Many of these different places on the continuum have their own identity labels (see *demiromantic*). Sometimes abbreviated to "aro" (pronounced like "arrow").

asexual: Not having sexual attraction or desire for other people.

binder: An undergarment used to alter or reduce the appearance of one's breasts (worn similarly to how one wears a sports bra).

biphobia: Prejudice, fear, or hatred directed toward bisexual people.

bisexual: Emotionally, romantically, or sexually attracted to more than one sex, gender, or gender identity, though not necessarily simultaneously, in the same way, or to the same degree.

cisgender: Sometimes shortened to "cis." A term used to describe a person whose gender identity aligns with that typically associated with the sex assigned to them at birth.

closeted: Describes an LGBTQ+ person who has not disclosed their sexual orientation or gender identity.

coming out: The process by which a person first acknowledges, accepts, and appreciates their sexual orientation or gender identity and begins to share that with others.

conversion therapy: Attempting to change a person's sexual orientation or gender identity through religious or psychological intervention.

cross-dresser: Someone who wears clothes of another gender/sex.

drag king: Someone who performs (hyper-)masculinity theatrically.

drag queen: Someone who performs (hyper-)femininity theatrically.

feminine-of-center; masculine-of-center: A phrase that indicates a range in terms of gender identity and expression for people who present, understand themselves, and/or relate to others in a generally more feminine/masculine way but don't necessarily identify as women or men. Feminine-of-center individuals may also identify as "femme," "submissive," "transfeminine," etc.; masculine-of-center individuals may also often identify as "butch," "stud," "aggressive," "boi," "transmasculine," etc.

femme: Someone who identifies themselves as feminine, whether it be physically, mentally, or emotionally. Often used to refer to a feminine-presenting queer person.

FtM / F2M: Female-to-male transgender or transsexual person.

gay: Emotionally, romantically, or sexually attracted to members of the same gender.

gender binary: The idea that there are only two genders and that every person is one of those two.

gender dysphoria: Clinically significant distress caused when a person's assigned birth gender is not the same as the one with which they identify. According to the American Psychiatric Association's *Diagnostic and Statistical Manual of Mental Disorders, 5th edition* (DSM-5), the term—which replaces "Gender Identity Disorder"—"is intended to better characterize the experiences of affected children, adolescents, and adults."

gender-expansive: Conveys a wider, more flexible range of gender identity and/or expression than typically associated with the binary gender system.

gender expression: External appearance of one's gender identity, usually expressed through behavior, clothing, haircut, or voice, and which may or may not conform to socially defined behaviors and characteristics typically associated with being either masculine or feminine.

genderfluid: Describes a person who does not identify with a single fixed gender, or expresses a fluid or unfixed gender identity.

gender identity: One's innermost concept of self as male, female, a blend of both, or neither; how individuals perceive themselves and what they call themselves. One's gender identity can be the same as or different from their sex assigned at birth.

gender nonconforming: A broad term referring to people who do not behave in a way that conforms to the traditional expectations of their gender, or whose gender expression does not fit neatly into a category.

genderqueer: Genderqueer people typically reject notions of static categories of gender and embrace a fluidity of gender identity and often, though not always, sexual orientation. People who identify as "genderqueer" may see themselves as both male and female, neither male nor female, or falling completely outside these categories.

gender transition: The process by which some people strive to more closely align their internal knowledge of gender with its outward appearance. Some people socially transition, whereby they might begin dressing, using names and pronouns, and/or being socially recognized as another gender. Others undergo physical transitions in which they modify their bodies through medical interventions.

heteronormativity: The assumption, in individuals and/or in institutions, that everyone is heterosexual and that heterosexuality is superior to all other sexualities. Leads to invisibility and stigmatizing of other sexualities. Example: when learning a woman is married, asking her what her husband's name is. Heteronormativity also leads us to assume that only masculine men and feminine women are straight.

homophobia: The fear and hatred of or discomfort with people who are attracted to members of the same sex.

homosexual: Primarily emotionally, physically, and/or sexually attracted to members of the same sex/gender. This medical term is considered stigmatizing (particularly as a noun) due to its historical use as a category of mental illness, and is generally discouraged for common use (use "gay" or "lesbian" instead).

intersex: An umbrella term used to describe a wide range of natural bodily variations. In some cases, these traits are visible at birth; in others, they are not apparent until puberty. Some chromosomal variations of this type may not be physically apparent at all.

lesbian: A woman who is emotionally, romantically, or sexually attracted to other women.

LGBTQ+: An abbreviation for "lesbian, gay, bisexual, transgender, and queer." Sometimes denoted with different or additional letters.

living openly: A state in which LGBTQ+ people are comfortably out about their sexual orientation or gender identity, where and when it feels appropriate to them.

MtF / M2F: male-to-female transgender or transsexual person.

nonbinary: Describes a person who does not identify exclusively as a man or a woman. Nonbinary people may identify as being both a man and a woman, somewhere in between, or falling completely outside these categories. While many also identify as transgender, not all nonbinary people do.

outing: Exposing someone's lesbian, gay, bisexual, or transgender identity to others without their permission. Outing someone can have serious repercussions on employment, economic stability, personal safety, and/or religious and family situations.

pansexual: Describes someone who has the potential for emotional, romantic, or sexual attraction to people of any gender, though not necessarily simultaneously, in the same way, or to the same degree.

passing: Trans people being accepted as, or able to "pass for," a member of their self-identified gender identity (regardless of sex assigned at birth) without being identified as trans.

QPOC / QTPOC: Abbreviations that stand for "queer people of color" and "queer and/or trans people of color."

queer: A term people often use to express fluid identities and orientations. Often used interchangeably with "LGBTQ+."

questioning: A term used to describe people who are in the process of exploring their sexual orientation or gender identity.

sex assigned at birth: The sex (male or female) given to a child at birth, most often based on the child's external anatomy. This is also referred to as "assigned sex at birth."

sexual orientation: An inherent or enduring emotional, romantic, or sexual attraction to other people.

trans: An umbrella term covering a range of identities that transgress socially defined gender norms. Trans with an asterisk is often used in written forms (not spoken) to indicate that you are referring to the larger group nature of the term, and specifically including nonbinary identities as well as transgender men and women.

transgender: An umbrella term for people whose gender identity and/or expression is different from cultural expectations based on the sex they were assigned at birth. Being transgender does not imply any specific sexual orientation. Therefore, transgender people may identify as straight, gay, lesbian, bisexual, etc.

transphobia: The fear and hatred of, or discomfort with, transgender people.

two-spirit: An umbrella term traditionally used within Native American communities to recognize individuals who possess qualities or fulfill roles of both genders.

ADDITIONAL RESOURCES

★ FINDING LOCAL LGBTQ+ COMMUNITIES

Aside from just Googling "LGBTQ+ communities near me," these resources can help you locate LGBTQ+ community centers in your area.

- ★ Scan college-campus maps to find local LGBTQ+ centers run by at least one professional staff or graduate assistant.

- ★ Everyone Is Gay: www.everyoneisgay.com. Check out their "Community and Activism" page under the Resources tab for advice on finding local communities for LGBTQ+ young adults.

- ★ Social CenterLink: The Community of LGBT Centers: www.lgbtcenters.org. Enter your address or location and find your nearest LGBTQ+ community center.

- ★ GSA Network: Your school, or a school near you, may have a Gay-Straight Alliance. Ask a school counselor or look on www.gsanetwork.org to locate a registered GSA near you.

- ★ Consortium of Higher Education: LGBT Resource Professionals. www.lgbtcampus.org/find-an-lgbt-campus-center

- ★ Media: Facebook, Instagram, or Tumblr can be good places to meet local LGBTQ+ people. However, always use caution and wisdom when talking to people online. Never meet up alone with someone you "met" online.

★ NATIONAL LGBTQ+ COMMUNITIES
(MOST PULLED FROM GLAAD.ORG/RESOURCELIST)

JUST FOR TEENS

- ★ The Trevor Project: leading national organization in crisis intervention, suicide prevention, resources, and support systems for LGBTQ+ youth.

- ★ It Gets Better Project: itgetsbetter.org. Inspiring stories from LGBTQ+ youth and adults.

- ★ The Tribe Wellness Community: www.support. therapytribe.com. Members: peer-to-peer support group for LGBTQ+ individuals dealing with mental health issues.

- ★ Gay, Lesbian & Straight Education Network (GLSEN): Find your local chapter or take a dive through their wonderful online resources.

- ★ LGBTQ+ Student Resources and Support: resource page on www.accreditedschoolsonline.org.

- ★ Point Foundation: www.pointfoundation.org. The national LGBTQ+ scholarship fund. Resources for rising college students.

- ★ Safe Schools Coalition: www.safeschoolscoalition. org. A public-private partnership to support LGBTQ+ youth.

FOR THE POLITICALLY PASSIONATE

- ★ Human Rights Campaign (HRC): www.hrc.org. Latest news, research, and resources on LGBTQ+ rights and activism.

- ★ Equality Federation: www.equalityfederation.org. An organization that partners with state-based organizations that advocate for LGBTQ+ people.

★ National LGBTQ+ Task Force: www.thetaskforce.org. Advocacy opportunities, news, conference updates, and more on LGBTQ+ rights.

BISEXUAL

★ BiNet USA: www.binetusa.org. America's oldest advocacy organization for bisexual, pansexual, fluid, queer-identified, and unlabeled people.

★ Bi.org: www.bi.org. All things bi here! Articles on famous bi people, Q&As, advice on coming out, and more.

★ Bisexual Resource Center: www.biresource.or.g

TRANSGENDER

★ National Center for Transgender Equality (NCTE): www.transequality.org. Resources, self-help guides, info about transgender people, and more.

★ Sylvia Rivera Law Project: www.srlp.org. Legal organization that fights discrimination based on sexuality, gender expression, race, income, etc.

★ Transgender Law Center: www.transgenderlawcenter.org.

★ Transgender Legal Defense & Education Fund: www.tledf.org.

ASEXUAL

★ The Asexual Visibility & Education Network: www. asexuality.org. An online community and archive of resources on asexuality.

★ The "Asexuality" tab on Pride Resource Center: https://prideresourcecenter.colostate.edu/resources/online-resources/asexuality/

- ★ "Intro to Asexuality" on Teen Health Source: http://teenhealthsource.com/blog/intro-to-asexuality/

ONLINE HANGOUTS

- ★ Empty Closets: www.emptyclosets.com. For age 13 and up. Coming-out resources and a safe place to chat.

- ★ TrevorSpace: www.trevorspace.org. For 13- to 24-year-olds. A monitored, international community of queer young people.

- ★ Q Christian Fellowship: www.qchristian.org. Has a safe, monitored online community for all your LGBTQ+ and faith questions.

- ★ Queer Grace: www.queergrace.com. An online encyclopedia for LGBTQ+ and Christian life. Has online support and communities. Includes a list of affirming Facebook, Twitter, and Tumblr.

- ★ Wattpad: www.wattpad.com. A social publishing platform where users share their written stories and fanfiction; allows LGBTQ+ people to connect through writing.

★ HOW TO FIND AN AFFIRMING CHURCH

When looking for an LGBTQ+-affirming church, know the right language. An LGBTQ+ "welcoming" or "friendly" church may be open and inclusive of LGBTQ+ people but may not necessarily be affirming. "Affirming" generally implies that the church/denomination does not believe homosexuality in any form to be a sin.

Make a short list (based on the list below) of possible affirming churches you're interested in. Look them up online and read their statement of faith or "what we believe" page (most churches will have this posted). You should be able to find their view on marriage, sexuality, etc. here.

Alternatively, send an email to the pastor of the church asking if they are LGBTQ+-affirming. If the response is not absolutely clear in it's affirming stance, you may want to look elsewhere.

WHERE TO START LOOKING

- ★ **www.gaychurch.org:** Largest directory of LGBTQ+-affirming churches and denominations. Enter your location or search their directory to find an affirming congregation near you.

- ★ **churchclarity.org:** Database of local congregations scored on how clearly they communicate their policies on LGBTQ+ inclusion.

LGBTQ+-AFFIRMING DENOMINATIONS, FAITH ORGANIZATIONS, ETC.

- ★ Affirm United/S'affirmer Ensemble (United Church of Canada)
- ★ Alliance of Baptists
- ★ American Apostolic Old Catholic Church
- ★ American Catholic Church
- ★ Anthem Network (Convergent Christian Communion)
- ★ Association of Welcoming and Affirming Baptists
- ★ Baptists Peace Fellowship
- ★ Brethren Mennonite Council for Lesbian and Gay Concerns
- ★ Christ Catholic Church
- ★ Communion of Synodal Catholic Churches
- ★ Covenant Network
- ★ Covenant Network of Presbyterians
- ★ Dignity USA (Catholic)

- ★ Ecumenical Catholic Communion
- ★ Evangelical Anglican Church in America
- ★ Evangelical Catholic Church
- ★ Friends for Lesbian, Gay, Bisexual, Transgender, and Queer Concerns (Quaker)
- ★ GALA: Gay and Lesbian Acceptance (Community of Christ)
- ★ GLAD Alliance (Disciples of Christ)
- ★ Inclusive Church UK (Anglican)
- ★ Independent Catholic Christian Church
- ★ Integrity (Episcopal)
- ★ Integrity in Canada (Anglican)
- ★ International Christian Community
- ★ Liberal Catholic Church
- ★ Metropolitan Community Churches
- ★ More Light Presbyterian (PCUSA)
- ★ New Ways Ministry (Catholic)
- ★ Orthodox-Catholic Church of America
- ★ Progressive Episcopal Church
- ★ Proud Anglicans of Canada
- ★ Reconciling Ministries Network (United Methodist Church)
- ★ Reconciling Pentecostals International
- ★ ReconcilingWorks: Lutherans for Full Participation (ELCA)
- ★ Reformed Catholic Church
- ★ Room for All

- ★ Seventh-Day Adventist Kinship International
- ★ The Evangelical Network (TEN) (Charismatic)
- ★ The National Catholic Church of America
- ★ UCC Coalition for LGBT Concerns (United Church of Christ)
- ★ Unitarian Universalist Association
- ★ United Catholic Church
- ★ United Church of Christ (not all welcoming)
- ★ Unity (Unity Ministries Worldwide)
- ★ Welcoming Community Network (Community of Christ)

★ BOOKS FOR LGBTQ+ TEENS
A FEW FUN ONES

- ★ *Simon vs. the Homo Sapiens Agenda.* Becky Albertali. In this ground-breaking, award-winning novel, 16-year-old Simon is outed through a misguided email and must leave his comfortable closet.

- ★ *The Art of Being Normal.* Lisa Williamson. The story of two transgender teens, Leo and Kate, at pivotal moments in their lives.

- ★ *Aristotle and Dante Discover the Secrets of the Universe.* Benjamin Alire Sáenz. One is an angry teen, the other a quirky know-it-all. Both are loners who discover a life-changing friendship in each other.

- ★ *All Out: The No-Longer-Secret Stories of Queer Teens throughout the Ages.* Edited by Saundra Mitchell. Seventeen young adults across the queer spectrum weave a collection of beautiful historical fiction for teens.

FOR YOUR FAITH (FULL LIST ON QUEERGRACE.COM)

★ *Bulletproof Faith: A Spiritual Survival Guide for Gay and Lesbian Christians.* Candace Chellew-Hodge. A practical guide for navigating the Christian LGBTQ+ minefield and cultivating a loving, defendable faith.

★ *Gay and Christian, No Contradiction.* Brandan Roberston. A boiled-down guide on reconciling Christianity and LGBTQ+ sexuality and identity.

★ *God and the Gay Christian: A Brief Guide for Reconciling Christian Faith and LGBTQ+ Identity.* Matthew Vines. Vines, a leading LGBTQ+ theologian, tackles the biggest questions about same-sex marriage, homosexuality, and Scripture.

★ *One Coin Found: How God's Love Stretches to the Margins.* Emmy Kegler. As a queer woman in both progressive and conservative churches, Kegler set out to fall in love with the Bible and become a minister.

★ *Transforming: The Bible and the Lives of Transgender Christians.* Austen Hartke. As a bisexual, transgender man, Hartke shares his experience with church and how to find a welcoming faith community.

★ *Radical Love: An Introduction to Queer Theology.* Patrick S. Cheng. For the intellectual seeking a full-fledged, yet accessible introduction to queer theology.

TRUE STORIES OF LGBTQ+ PEOPLE

★ *Queer There and Everywhere.* Sarah Prager. Written just for LGBTQ+ youth, this book tells the story of 23 queer and trans people who changed history.

★ *Oranges Are Not the Only Fruit.* Jeanette Winterson. A young, spunky girl is adopted by a surly Pentecostal family and grows into her "unorthodox" sexuality.

* *Boy Erased.* Garrard Conley. The haunting memoir of Conley's fundamentalist childhood and experience through conversion therapy.

* *Tomorrow Will Be Different.* Sarah McBride. The first transgender person to speak at a national political convention, McBride writes of love, loss, and her fight for equal rights.

* *Sissy: A Coming-of-Gender Story.* Jacob Tobia. A comical, yet brutally honest memoir about growing up and discovering if you're (a) a boy, (b) a girl, (c) something in between, or (d) all of the above.

★ MENTAL HEALTH

10 Common Warning Signs of a Mental Health Condition: https://www.nami.org/NAMI/media/NAMI-Media/Infographics/NAMI-Getting-the-Right-Start.pdf

1. for more than two weeks, feeling sad or experiencing lack of desire to be around others

2. seriously considering or making plans to harm or kill oneself

3. out-of-control, risky behavior

4. sudden, overwhelming fear for no rational reason

5. appetite suppression, throwing up or using laxatives to lose weight; significant weight loss or weight gain

6. seeing, hearing, or believing things that aren't real

7. consistently using drugs or alcohol

8. drastic mood changes, behavioral or personality swings, or poor sleeping habits

9. extreme difficulty concentrating or staying still

10. intense worries or fears that inhibit daily activity

WHO SHOULD YOU TELL?

- ★ family member
- ★ close friend
- ★ teacher or professor
- ★ counselor or coach
- ★ faith leader

WHAT SHOULD YOU DO/SAY?

- ★ Talk to your primary care doctor to rule out any other physical health conditions.
- ★ Be honest about how you're feeling and how you want to feel.
- ★ Ask for help finding a therapist, counselor, or mental health specialist.
- ★ https://www.nami.org/NAMI/media/NAMI-Media/Infographics/NAMI-Taking-Charge-of-Your-Mental-Health.pdf

MENTAL HEALTH BOOKS FOR TEENS

- ★ *Feeling Better: A CBT Workbook for Teens*. Rachel L. Hutt, PhD. Essential skills and activities to help you manage moods, boost self-esteem, and conquer anxiety.
- ★ *Just as You Are: A Teen's Guide to Self-Acceptance & Lasting Self-Esteem*. Michelle Skeen, PsyD. Kelly Skeen.
- ★ *Don't Let Your Emotions Run Your Life for Teens: Dialectical Behavior Therapy Skills for Helping You Manage Mood Swings, Control Angry Outbursts, and Get Along with Others*. Sheri Van Dijk, MSW. Highly recommended book by adolescent therapists.

* *The Anxiety and Phobia Workbook.* Edward Bourne, PhD. A guide through understanding and dealing with anxiety, OCD, and PTSD.

* *My Anxious Mind: A Teen's Guide to Managing Anxiety and Panic.* Michael A. Tompkins, PhD, and Katherine A. Martinez, PsyD, illustrated by Michael Sloan.

FICTION BOOKS ABOUT TEEN MENTAL ILLNESS

* *Turtles All the Way Down* by John Green

* *Challenger Deep* by Neal Shusterman

* *Free Verse* by Sarah Dooley

* *Paperweight* by Meg Haston

* *History Is All You Left Me* by Adam Silvera

* *When We Collided* by Emery Lord

* *Fangirl* by Rainbow Rowell

★ SUICIDAL THOUGHTS

If you or someone you know is having thoughts of suicide, please get help immediately. Here are a few hotlines with free, professional help for LGBTQ+ teens and adults.

* National Suicide Hotline: 1-800-273-8255. Free, confidential support for any age at any time, 24/7.

* Crisis Text Line: Text "HOME" to 741741

* Trevor Project: 1-866-488-7386. The nation's leading organization for crisis intervention and suicide prevention specifically for LGBTQ+ young people under 25. 24/7 support line.

* Trans Lifeline: translifeline.org or call 877-565-8860. A national trans-led organization dedicated to improving the quality of trans lives.

- ★ Crisis Text Line: Text START to 741-741 to message 24/7 with a trained crisis counselor.
- ★ LGBTQ+ National Youth Talkline. email: help@LGBThotline.org

IF YOU OR SOMEONE YOU KNOW IS CONSIDERING NON-SUICIDAL SELF-HARM:

- ★ Self-Abuse Finally Ends (S.A.F.E.): 800-DONTCUT (800-366-8288) offers local support and therapy referrals as well as immediate support.

★ HOW TO FIND A THERAPIST/COUNSELOR

Brief Guide to Finding the Right Counselor

- ★ Ask friends for referrals or search online.

- ★ Read online profiles well; look for therapists who are LGBTQ+ or specialize in that field.

- ★ Make sure your counselor or therapist is certified. Look for "LPC" (licensed professional counselor), "LCSW" or "LSW" (licensed clinical social worker or licensed social worker). Other acronyms indicating certification in specific fields include LEP, LPCC, LMFT, LCP. Verify credentials on the Department of Consumer Affairs website for your state.

- ★ Check if or which types of therapy may be covered by your health insurance.

- ★ There are many types and approaches to therapy. Make sure you know which one you're going to. If you don't like it, find a therapist with a different approach.

- ★ Set up a consultation or screening call before setting up an appointment. Ask questions that are important for you to find the right therapist.

- ⭐ Keep in mind the first session is always a bit awkward. Make sure they respect your boundaries, give you their full attention, and actively listen.

- ⭐ After a few weeks, you should feel supported and encouraged after counseling. If your therapist/counselor just doesn't feel like a good fit, leave and try a different one.

- ⭐ Warning signs: therapist constantly checking watch, guilting you for quitting, threatening a spiral of depression if you stop therapy, therapist talking more than you, interrupting you often, sexually or emotionally inappropriate behavior, violation of confidentiality (the last two are reportable offenses).

ONLINE COUNSELING RESOURCES

- ⭐ The Christian Closet: www.thechristiancloset.com. The first fully LGBTQ+ team of counselors, coaches, and spiritual directors providing 100% online mental and spiritual health services.

- ⭐ 7 Cups: www.7cups.org. Affordable online therapy, 24/7 chat, self-help guides, and more.

- ⭐ www.pridecounseling.com. Fill out info about your orientation/identity and get matched with a licensed therapist. Messaging with your therapist is according to your schedule.

- ⭐ www.goodtherapy.com. Check here for licensed counselors with LGBTQ+ experience or education.

- ⭐ Psychology Today: www.psychologytoday.com. Check out their "Finding a Gay Therapist" section and enter your city or ZIP code.

★ The Tribe Wellness Community: www.support.therapytribe.com. Members. Peer-to-peer support group for LGBTQ+ individuals dealing with mental health issues.

LOCAL RESOURCES

★ Check if your local LGBTQ+ community has staff therapists or knows of good local counselors.

★ Ask your pastor or faith leader if they know of affirming counselors/therapists in your area.

★ Ask your primary care doctor for referrals.

★ Talk to a school counselor and ask for recommendations for therapists/counselors.

REVIEWS ON THERAPISTS

Check these sites for therapist reviews in your area:

★ www.goodtherapy.org: "Find the Right Therapist"

★ www.yelp.com —yes, that's right. Yelp can be a decently reliable resource for local therapist/counselor reviews.

★ www.healthgrades.com: A site to review doctors, hospitals, and mental health specialists. Reliable, but doctors can remove up to two reviews of their choice.

★ SUBSTANCE ABUSE

RECOGNIZING SUBSTANCE ABUSE

The first step in getting help for substance abuse is recognizing that it's happening. Addiction can happen to anyone at any time and can manifest in a variety of ways:

★ hanging out with different friends

★ not caring about your appearance

* getting worse grades in school

* missing classes or skipping school

* losing interest in your favorite activities

* getting in trouble in school or with the law

* having different eating or sleeping habits

* having more problems with family members and friends

WHEN CONSIDERING THE BEST TREATMENT FOR YOU

* Know that treatments are all different and unique to each person.

* Know that quitting substance abuse is extremely difficult, even if you want to.

* You'll likely go through a "detox" as your body adjusts to an absence of drugs. Please do this under professional, medical supervision. Symptoms may include depression, anxiety, and other mood disorders, as well as restlessness and sleeplessness. Treatment centers will keep you safe and comfortable through this process.

* Remember, relapsing doesn't mean that treatment failed. People with many other health conditions (like asthma or high blood pressure) relapse as much as people with an addiction.

* Treatment requires major, often difficult lifestyle changes. Setbacks are to be expected. Keep persevering through them and consider a different treatment method to replace unsuccessful methods.

* Know that your treatment providers will keep your information confidential. They are not under

obligation to tell your parents or law enforcement about your drug use *unless you are in danger of harming yourself or someone else.*

TO FIND IMMEDIATE HELP

★ PRIDE Institute: 888-616-5031. https://pride-institute.com/ Recovery programs provide solutions for all types of substance abuse, trauma, sexual and behavioral issues.

★ SAMHSA (Substance Abuse and Mental Health Services Administration): 1-800-662-HELP (4357). Free, confidential, 24/7, 365-day-a-year treatment referral and information service for individuals and families facing mental and/or substance use disorders.

FOR LONG-TERM OR INPATIENT HELP

★ Tell your parents and ask for their support. Have them read articles such as the parent helps on drugabuse.gov.

★ Talk to your doctor about what's going on. They can help you explore different treatment options.

★ With your parents and your doctor, decide if a treatment facility is right for you.

★ Consider getting counseling or other behavioral treatment options.

★ Ask your treatment provider if support groups or programs such as Alcoholics Anonymous, Narcotics Anonymous, or Cocaine Anonymous may be a right choice for you.

* To find support groups in your area, contact local hospitals, treatment centers, or faith-based organizations.

* Find more information at teen.drugabuse.gov.

★ SEXUAL HEALTH AND EDUCATION
FOR INFORMATION ON MARRIAGE, SEXUALITY, ETC. FROM AN LGBTQ+ PERSPECTIVE.

* David and Constantino Khalaf, *Modern Kinship: A Queer Guide to Christian Marriage*. From dating without smartphone apps to meeting the in-laws to deciding to have kids, *Modern Kinship* encourages queer Christians desiring a God-centered partnership or marriage.

* Bromleigh McCleneghan, *Good Christian Sex: Why Chastity Isn't the Only Option—and Other Things the Bible Says about Sex*. A shame- and guilt-free look at sexuality in a Christian context.

* Dianna Anderson, *Damaged Goods: New Perspectives on Christian Purity*. Provocative and engaging, Anderson will change the way you look at sex, abstinence, politics, and faith.

* Margaret Farley, *Just Love: A Framework for Christian Sexual Ethics*. One of America's leading ethicists argues for sexual ethics where justice and love are the center.

HELP FOR SEXUAL ABUSE OR SEXUAL HEALTH
HOTLINES, HELPLINES, ETC.

* RAINN (Rape, Abuse & Incest National Network). The nation's largest anti-sexual violence organization. Call their free, confidential hotline at 800-656-HOPE (4673).

- ★ GLBTQ Domestic Violence Project: 800-832-1901. Website, info, and hotline for LGBTQ+ victims of domestic violence and their families.

- ★ The Network/La Red: 617-742-4911: Emotional support, information, and safety planning for those being partner-abused or who have been abused in the LGBTQ+ community, as well as sadomasochism or polyamorous communities.

- ★ National Teen Dating Abuse Helpline: 1-866-331-9474.

- ★ National Domestic Violence Hotline: 1-800-799-7233 or 1-800-7870-3224 (TTY).

- ★ National Coalition of Anti-Violence Programs: 1-212-714-1141. Links to National Advocacy for Local LGBT Communities.

- ★ National AIDS Hotline: English: 1-800-342-2437. Spanish: 1-800-344-7432. TTY service for the deaf: 1-800-243-7889.

- ★ Love Is Respect: 1-866-331-9474 or text loveis to 22522. https://www.loveisrespect.org/

RESOURCES FOR DEALING WITH SEXUAL ABUSE

- ★ DayOne: Partnering with youth to end dating abuse and domestic violence. Additional resources for LGBTQ+ youth struggling with partner abuse. https://www.dayoneny.org/

- ★ NCTSN (The National Child Traumatic Stress Network): Find resources on sexual abuse, the effects, interventions, and help at www.nctsn.org.

- ★ "It's Never Your Fault: The Truth about Sexual Abuse" at https://www.nctsn.org/resources/its-never-your-fault-truth-about-sexual-abuse.

- ★ 1in6.org: National helpline for men who were sexually abused or assaulted.

- ★ VAWnet (Violence Against Women): A project of the National Resource Center on Domestic Violence.

- ★ Invisible Girls Thrive: www.invisiblegirlsthrive. org. Honors teen girls and young women who have survived incest and all sexual abuse through "thriverships," opportunity, and education.

RESOURCES FOR SEX EDUCATION

- ★ Planned Parenthood: www.plannedparenthood.org. Resources for sexual health, reproductive health, and much more. Check out their LGBTQ+ section under the "Teen" tab.

- ★ Scarleteen: Sex Ed for the Real World. www.scarleteen.com

- ★ Sex. Etc. www.sexetc.org. An online resource for sex ed just for teens. Blogs, magazines, fun articles, and an action center to find health resources and know your rights.

- ★ Center for Young Women's Health: www.youngwomenshealth.org

- ★ Young Men's Health: www.youngmenshealthsite.org

- ★ Trans Youth Sexual Health Booklet

- ★ "Queering Sexual Education" on www.teenhealthsource.com. Article and video links for sex ed for queer teens.

- ★ Queer Sex Ed: www.queersexed.org.

★ IF YOU'RE AT RISK OF HOMELESSNESS

FOR IMMEDIATE HELP

- ★ The National Runaway Safeline: 1-800-RUNAWAY (800-786-2929). Provides advice and resources, like shelter, transportation, assistance in finding counseling, and transitioning back to home life. Frontline staff will also act as advocates and mediators if/as needed.

- ★ True Colors United: Working to end homelessness specifically among LGBTQ+ teens. https://truecolorsunited.org/. (212)-461-4401

HOW TO FIND LOCAL RESOURCES

- ★ National Safe Place: www.nationalsafeplace.org. Click on their "Find a Safe Place" tab to enter your ZIP code and find local help. To use TXT 4 HELP, text the word "safe" and your current location (city/state/ZIP) to 4HELP (44357). You will receive a message with the closest Safe Place site and phone number for the local youth agency. You will also have the option to text interactively with a professional for more help. It's quick, easy, safe, and confidential.

- ★ National Clearinghouse on Homeless Youth & Families: 833-GET-RHYi (833-438-7494) or GetRHYi@NCHYF.org. NCHYF has connections with the following programs and can help you find local resources.

- ★ Basic Center Program: Provides up to 21 days of shelter, food, clothing, and medical care; individual, group, and family counseling; crisis intervention, recreation programs, and aftercare services for teens under 18.

* Transitional Living Program (TLP): provides long-term residential services to homeless youth between the ages of 16 and 22. Housing may be in host families, supervised apartments, group homes (or maternity group homes). Offers educational and life skills programs.

* SAMSHA's resources for homelessness: https://www.samhsa.gov/homelessness-programs-resources